"SOMETHING THERE IS THAT DOESN'T LOVE A WALL..."
—*Robert Frost*

From tense Berlin, from Tokyo to Djakarta and Bandung in Indonesia, wherever walls of misunderstanding divide to conquer, the vigorous message of the Free World was carried to the hearts and minds of people around the world by Attorney General and Mrs. Robert F. Kennedy . . .

"We have no infallible party, no iron creed, no all-purpose blueprint; we do not propose to chain mankind to a system of false logic. We have, instead, faith in human intelligence, human will and human decency; and we know that, in the long run, these are the forces which make history."

JUST FRIENDS AND BRAVE ENEMIES was originally published at $3.95 by Harper and Row, Publishers.

BEYOND THE WALLS THAT MEN

BUILD AGAINST OTHER MEN ...

There was Berlin:
"Suddenly my talk was interrupted by loud explosions as the Communists set off two rockets. They soared directly over the square and burst in the sky above us ... The crowd booed and hissed in anger ..."

There was Tokyo:
"We had eaten snails and seaweed for breakfast and whale meat for lunch. We had slept on floors, lived through an earthquake ... We had learned a great deal and enjoyed ourselves tremendously ..."

This is the fascinating, often humorous personal story of the Kennedys' trip.

"We must meet our duty
and convince the world that we are

JUST FRIENDS
AND
BRAVE ENEMIES"

—Thomas Jefferson

By ROBERT F. KENNEDY

POPULAR LIBRARY • NEW YORK
NED L. PINES—*President*
FRANK P. LUALDI—*Publisher*

POPULAR LIBRARY EDITION
Published in February, 1963

Published by arrangement with Harper & Row, Publishers
Harper & Row edition published in August, 1962

Public speeches and documents included in this book are in the public domain.

Cover photo: Wide World Photo

To Ethel—RUTH, I:16-7
And to my mother and father,
whose nine children owe a debt which
can never be repaid

CONTENTS

CHAPTER 1

"The World Is a Proud Place"

> ". . . the world is a proud place, peopled with men
> of positive quality . . . who will not let us sleep."
> —EMERSON, *Society and Solitude*

In 1951, President Kennedy, then Congressman Kennedy of
the Eleventh District of Massachusetts, my sister Pat and I
arrived in Tokyo, three dusty travelers on the last leg of a
trip which had taken us around the world.

We had visited many countries—Pakistan, India, Thailand,
Malaya, and what was then called Indo-China. We had seen
the beauty of the temples of Bangkok; the poverty that
plagued India; the fighting and killing that gripped Indo-
China.

In some nations it was a time of terror and intrigue. In
Pakistan we met Prime Minister Liaquat Ali Khan—and
three days after we saw him he was slain by an assassin.
We traveled through Kuala Lumpur, but because of the
guerrilla fighting we did so in a British tank.

We saw the Foreign Legion and the French paratroopers
in their bright red berets, and we felt even then that many
of them were doomed.

And with all of this behind us—the beauty, the chaos and
death—we looked forward to our visit in Japan.

I can think of nothing so harassing for people assigned to
foreign capitals as the duties of arranging programs and accommodations for visiting dignitaries.

We were, of course, pretty far down on the list of important visitors. As we stepped from the plane, I could almost
hear the Second Secretary say to the Third Secretary: "Can

you believe it? A Congressman is already bad enough. But this one had to bring his sister and his brother. What can we do with all of them?"

What they did with us on our arrival was turn us over to Dr. Gunji Hosono, the Director of the Japan Institute of Foreign Affairs. And Dr. Hosono was very kind to us. He had been in England when my father was Ambassador to the Court of St. James's many years before, and he had remembered our family. He went out of his way to make us feel at home in Japan. He made our visit to Tokyo most rewarding.

After our departure he followed up his kindness to us with many other acts of friendship. When my mother visited Japan some years later he welcomed her and made certain that she was taken care of. And still later he looked after my other sisters on their travels through the Far East.

Frequently he corresponded with us. In 1952, when Congressman Kennedy was running for the United States Senate, it was Dr. Hosono who located Commander Hanami, the Commanding Officer of the Japanese destroyer which had split PT 109 in half in the Pacific in World War II. In fact, he arranged for Commander Hanami to write a letter praising and endorsing Congressman Kennedy during the course of that election campaign. It was rather unusual, but it helped.

When Senator Kennedy became President Kennedy he remembered Dr. Hosono and invited him to the Inauguration. And as the Inaugural Parade marched by, the President brought Dr. Hosono and his pretty daughter, Haruko, up to the reviewing stand to join him and Mrs. Kennedy for a brief period.

A short time later Dr. Hosono paid me a visit in the Department of Justice. He wanted the President to come to Japan and if that was impossible he was anxious for me to make a visit. It was essential, he said, for Japan to know about the New Frontier. He said the anti-American riots of 1960 had left a bad impression in Japan as well as in the United States and that most of his countrymen shared a very warm feeling for my country. He felt it would be most valuable if some gesture were made by a representative of the United States—a gesture which would have special appeal for the young people and the political liberals of Japan.

I explained that with my new responsibilities such a trip would be most difficult. He departed disappointed but not discouraged. He enlisted Ambassador Reischauer in his efforts. And he didn't stop there.

Every few weeks I would receive a letter stressing the importance of a trip to his country, and about every ten days a visitor from Japan would arrive in my office, armed with an introduction from Dr. Hosono. He would shake hands and sit down and immediately begin to urge that I go to Japan as soon as possible.

In the spring of 1961 when Ambassador Edwin Reischauer arrived in the United States I met with him and Secretary of State Dean Rusk at the White House. We discussed the possibility of my making such a trip, and Secretary Rusk advised that it should be early in 1962. He also suggested that I visit Indonesia. Few United States officials had been there, and a number of dignitaries of Communist countries, including Khrushchev, had made extended tours in President Sukarno's country.

Indonesia was on our itinerary in 1951. It had just gained its independence, and its public officials mistrusted white foreigners. Red tape, heat and humidity were my superficial impressions of a brief stay. This nation stretches across three thousand miles of islands along the belt of the Equator. It is the fifth largest nation in the world, with 96 million people. (The United States is fourth largest.) It is most important as a powerful leader of Southeast Asia and has tremendous potential—for good or for evil.

Indonesia is still struggling for control over its future and striving to determine its own destiny. It gained independence by blood and tears and now by sweat and toil is trying to retain it. There have been many problems in its relationship to the United States—at the same time the Soviet Union and the Communist bloc countries have been increasingly focusing their attention on it. The U.S.S.R. alone has furnished some $800 million in credits for aid to Indonesia; the United States aid has been only a fraction of this amount.

And while the United States staunchly supported Indonesian independence from Holland during the late 1940's, it was charged that in 1957 the United States gave at least token backing to an internal revolutionary force which tried to unseat President Sukarno and overthrow his government.

The Indonesian Government officials believed this to be true and understandably did not take it very kindly.

The Communists, both Russian and Chinese, have realized the importance of this new nation. Capture of Indonesia by the Communists would enable them to flank the whole of Southeast Asia, an area barely holding onto freedom by its fingertips. Not only would such an achievement have worldwide implications; it would give to the Communists tremendous natural resources of oil and rubber.

For despite an economy which is presently tilting on the brink of disaster, Indonesia has tremendous economic potential. Financial and economic mismanagement rather than lack of natural resources has been the cause of Indonesia's present plight. The average yearly income of the Indonesian is still approximately sixty dollars; fifteen cents a day is a good wage, when it could and should be many times this amount. Some elements of the Indonesian leadership have proved to be better revolutionary leaders than peacetime administrators.

With this untapped potential, it is, therefore, not surprising to find within Indonesia one of the strongest Communist parties outside the bloc. And at the time our visit was discussed they and their fellow citizens, non-Communists, Moslems and Christians, uneducated and educated, were thinking of only one issue—the status of West Irian or West New Guinea.

When Indonesia obtained its independence from the Netherlands in 1949, there was a last-minute dispute about how West New Guinea, then under Dutch control, should be handled. The discussions had advanced so far on all the other matters that, in the anxiety on both sides to resolve the over-all dispute, it was decided to put the West New Guinea issue aside, with both the Dutch and Indonesians committing themselves to resolving the question within a year. Instead, this dispute has dragged on for thirteen years. The relationship between the Dutch and Indonesians has steadily deteriorated. Dutch property was seized, diplomatic relations were discontinued. Finally, at the end of 1961 and in early 1962, the Indonesians indicated that they would take West New Guinea by force if it wasn't turned over to them peacefully. By this time the Dutch had made a commitment to the 700,000 Papuans who inhabit West New Guinea that they could determine for themselves what their future would be. The Indonesians argued that the Dutch had spent the intervening years poisoning the minds of the Papuans against the Indonesians. "Let us have a plebiscite," they said, "but until this is arranged we should be permitted to control the administration of West New Guinea." Each week that went by in 1962 saw a slow worsening of the situation.

Meanwhile, the Communist party within Indonesia was vocal in its demands for immediate military action. The anti-Communist elements within Indonesia realized the danger in this course of action. The Communist bloc countries, led by Russia and China, favored the Indonesians in this dispute. They were counted upon to supply men, matériel, planes and guns. As the Communists saw it, if hostilities were begun by Indonesia, the West, including the United States, would end up on the side of the Dutch, opposing the military action of the Indonesians. The lineup would then be described as a struggle between the colonial nations, supported by the United States, against the new nations of the world, supported by the Communists. This was a conflict which would be unpleasant at best and would, over an extended period of time, be virtually impossible for us to win. The Communists would become far more entrenched in Indonesia, the anti-Communists would have their position undermined, and Southeast Asia would have been encircled by the Soviet Union and China. For these reasons the United States was vitally interested in the results of the dispute.

By the time I went to Indonesia, however, the situation had deteriorated so badly that the opposing parties would not even talk to one another. My role therefore was not only to exhibit goodwill toward the millions of people of this new nation but to make every effort to persuade the Indonesian leadership of the importance of resolving this matter peacefully in discussions with the Dutch.

It was against this background that our trip to Japan and Indonesia was arranged. One more major stop, West Germany, was added.

In the fall of 1961 I received an invitation from Mayor Willy Brandt to give the Ernst Reuter Lecture at the Free University of Berlin. General Lucius Clay wrote from Berlin and later came to see me in Washington to urge such a visit. Some show of U.S. support was needed, he said. Berlin was

15

the most torn and tortured city of the world. West Berlin was a fortress of freedom. Vice-President Johnson's earlier visit had lifted the sagging morale of a tired but determined people, but General Clay felt our manifestations of support shouldn't stop there. Secretary Rusk agreed that a visit at the appropriate time would mean much in reaffirming our resolution to remain firm in West Berlin. Thus, I accepted Mayor Brandt's invitation to give the lecture in memory of Ernst Reuter, the late Mayor, whose genius and love of freedom had been largely responsible for Berlin's remaining free and non-Communist during the difficult airlift days.

There were to be the three major stops, and I will have more to say about each of these visits in the course of the book. But first I would like to say that this book is not a travelogue, nor is it meant to give the inside story on American foreign policy or our country's relationships with other countries as seen by the New Frontier. And, furthermore, I am not attempting to repeat here conversations held with the leaders of various countries. Full reports on all those discussions were made verbally and in writing to President Kennedy and Secretary Rusk, and obviously that is where they should end. This book, then, is rather a report on the kinds of questions that were asked and the kinds of problems that are troubling people in the lands we visited. I had an opportunity to talk with a great many people from extremely varied backgrounds, frequently under unusual circumstances, and these pages describe those meetings. This is a report on what happened, with the conversations frequently being a verbatim or abridged version of transcripts recorded in each instance by the United States Information Agency. And it is a summing up of some heightened impressions of our own country which served to reinforce my opinion that in certain crucial areas we must make a greater effort to fulfill our role in our own society and to live up to our ideals.

We decided to leave Washington on the first leg of the trip—to Japan, with a brief stop at Hawaii—on February 1, 1962. The party consisted of John Seigenthaler, my administrative assistant in the Justice Department, Brandon Grove, Jr., of the State Department, my wife Ethel and myself. We were also accompanied by about ten reporters and photographers sent by the news media to cover the trip. We traveled by commercial aircraft.

After the basic three-country itinerary was established, other visits were added by the State Department.

Our first stop after Japan was Taiwan, and we made a brief tour of part of that island.

We then spent a day and a half in Hong Kong, where we visited the refugee centers and met some of the 1,500,000 exiles who at that time had fled from Communist China to the free city of Hong Kong. I thought as I walked among these poor people that this was truly another illustration of the bankruptcy of the Communist system. With such evidence as this it is difficult to understand how the Communists could be as successful as they have been in portraying their system as the wave of the future and their form of government as one which improves the life of the individual. Visiting with these poor, emaciated, beaten people with their bewildered children was an experience I cannot forget.

Since we visited Hong Kong this situation has become much more tragic as thousands of starving Chinese, most of them very old or very young, flooded across the boundary of Red China in an effort to find food and a better life among this city's more than three million Oriental residents. During the first three weeks in May, following our visit in February, more than sixty thousand sought refuge in Hong Kong. Already in Red China the flow from Communism to freedom—which had so embarrassed the authorities in East Germany was being repeated.

After Hong Kong we had a very brief visit in Singapore. There I was asked about race relations in the United States and our position in the dispute between the Dutch and the Indonesians, as well as some questions about the alleged influence of gangsters in American life.

We then flew to Indonesia, and our first stop after leaving Djakarta was a short layover at Saigon in Vietnam, where guerrilla warfare, kidnapings, bombings and murder threatened to destroy the country. President Diem's brother came out to meet the plane, and a number of our own officials, military and civilian, also came out to the airport. Far from home, they fully realized the possibility that Southeast Asia might explode in the near future. It was clear that they wondered if the people in the United States knew. In a brief statement to the press about the struggle under way in Vietnam, I made the point that this is a new kind of war. It is war in the very real sense of the word, yet it is a war fought not by massive devisions but secretly by terror, assassination, ambush and infiltration. I added that the President "has been extremely impressed with the courage and determination of the people of your country and he has pledged the United States to stand by the side of Vietnam through this very difficult and troublesome time. We will win in Vietnam and we shall remain here until we do."

Our next stop was Thailand. Originally, the Department of State had suggested that in making the trip from the Far East to Europe I might stop in Iran. However, this plan was later changed and, because of the problem facing all Southeast Asia, it was decided that I should visit Thailand instead. Thus, a day was scheduled in that country. In view of developments which have since occurred there I am glad Thailand was included. There was deep concern even then that the turmoil of Laos would spill over into Thailand, and, if guerrillas and assassins began to infiltrate the Thai border, the questions in the minds of the officials of Thailand were whether the United States would assist them, and whether our allies in Europe also would be willing to assist. They have since received proof of our willingness. I went to Thailand, therefore, not only as a visitor but as an unofficial courier bearing a message from the President and the Secretary of State reinforcing what they had already been told by our Ambassador Young: that we in the United States were determined to help peoples and countries who were ready to help themselves. We considered the Thais our good friends; we realized that they were willing to make sacrifices—if necessary, to shed their blood for their freedom, and we wanted them to understand that we would meet our commitments and stand by them.

I carried this message to the Prime Minister and to the Foreign Minister. With them, and later with the King, I discussed the problems of the northeast section of their country and the possibility of military action in the future. It is the poorest section of Thailand, with no natural resources, and the people are ripe for subversion.

I had a short visit with some of the student leaders

in Bangkok. They too wanted to know whether the United States would stand by them, and they also asked the inevitable questions about civil rights.

While in Bangkok we took some time off to visit the silk looms where the colorful Thai silk is produced and dyed. It was necessary for us to board small paddle boats to cross a murky, sewage-filled canal. As the boats crossed the canal, one of the USIS men, standing in the bow of his boat, lost his balance and was dunked up to the neck, soaking John Seigenthaler in the process. He came dripping out of the sewage, his clothes drenched. He went home to change. When the story of our visit to the silk plants was reported by USIS I noted a slight degree of censorship. His splash was not mentioned.

The longest night of our trip came on February 20. After the stop at Bangkok we were to fly to Rome. The night flight began at 11:30 P.M. and arrival time in Rome was at 9:45 the next morning with a six-hour change in time. This meant a trip of over fifteen hours. The early morning refueling stops en route to Rome included Calcutta, Karachi and Beirut. At each stop press conferences were scheduled and a number of people from the American Embassies came to greet us.

At Calcutta we alighted at midnight and found our Ambassador to India, John Kenneth Galbraith, and his wife waiting for us at the plane steps. We had last seen Ken Galbraith in Hawaii, when we were on our way to Japan. He had been recuperating from an attack which had first been thought to be hepatitis and amoebic dysentery, but which subsequently proved to be less serious. While in Honolulu we went sailing and our boat capsized, causing as many headlines as a major naval disaster. I later received a telegram from Galbraith, making an ungallant comparison to my brother's adventures on PT 109. The message said:

SAILBOAT DISASTER CONTINUES TO BE MAJOR TOPIC OF COMMENT HERE. WOULD IT BE HELPFUL IF I SAID YOU WERE CUT DOWN BY A RUSSIAN DESTROYER KNIFING HER WAY INTO PEARL HARBOR AND THAT YOU SAVED YOUR ENTIRE CREW?

JUST FRIENDS AND BRAVE ENEMIES

With the Galbraiths was Arthur Schlesinger, who was abroad on a special assignment for the President. Perhaps thirty or forty of the Americans stationed in Calcutta and a good number of the Indian- and English-language press were on hand as well. Mr. and Mrs. Schlesinger joined us there and traveled on with us as far as Berlin. (It led my wife to write Ken Galbraith later that Jackie Kennedy went to India and received silks, valuable stones, an elephant and two tiger cubs and we went to India and got Arthur Schlesinger.)

American citizens also awaited us at Karachi, in Pakistan, where we arrived at 3:30 A.M., and at Beirut, where we put down at five in the morning.

We had not expected to be met at the airports in these foreign cities at such an inconvenient time of the morning— except by newsmen, who never seem to sleep. For the most part our stops were only for an hour. And yet these Americans left their beds and their homes and went out of their way to come out to shake hands. We were very grateful.

In Calcutta and Karachi I was struck, even on these short stops, by the difficulties that close neighbors have in getting along with one another.

In Calcutta the main theme of the questioning was why we were friendly with President Ayub of Pakistan, who was described as a dictator and not interested in democracy. On the other hand, in Karachi I was asked why we were friendly with Nehru, who had not been particularly friendly toward the United States and who would not permit self-determination for the people of Kashmir. There was bitterness in the voices of the reporters at both stops. It made me think how fortunate we were in having as neighbors Canada on the north and Mexico on the south.

In Karachi I expressed my appreciation for the friendship of Pakistan and all the help that that country and its people had rendered during the war in Korea. I told them the President was gratefully aware that in the difficulties of Southeast Asia, Pakistan, more than any other country, was willing to stand beside the United States and fight if necessary.

After a few more hours of flight we arrived in Beirut at dawn. I had an opportunity to see the American University once again. I think this institution, founded in 1866 by Protestant missionaries, has dramatically demonstrated the effect

20

a small group can have on history and the shape of the future. More world leaders have been educated at the American University of Beirut than at any other institution I can think of—even Harvard. This has been true for many years. There were more graduates of the American University of Beirut at the establishment of the United Nations than from any other institution. It has had a tremendously good effect internationally and has been a great credit to the United States.

By the time we arrived in Rome everybody was exhausted. All of us, the newspapermen and our party, consumed an enormous Italian lunch of *fettuccini* and then went to bed at five in the afternoon and slept until eight o'clock the next morning.

I had useful visits with Premier Fanfani as well as Italian Foreign Minister Segni. A new government in Italy was about to be formed, so it was an interesting time of transition. They were both concerned about the outlook of the young people in the countries of the Far East. We also discussed the role the Common Market would have among newly independent nations.

I wouldn't have thought it possible, but we had still another Roman luncheon, even more enormous than the first, climaxed by Ethel's being given a Vespa. It was the gift of the reporters and photographers who had been with us on the trip and who had already done so much to make it pleasant. In a final burst of enthusiasm they persuaded Ethel to start the thing up, and next we knew she was orbiting the small square outside the restaurant, frightening a sizable part of Rome's population and snarling its traffic pattern as far as the Colosseum.

While we were in Rome Colonel Glenn made his historic orbital flight. All Rome was alive with excitement. It was clear that this event had an immense effect on reinforcing America's position in the world.

We had a friendly audience with Pope John. He was also greatly pleased with Colonel Glenn's success. He is an impressive man, with a wonderful humility and a fine sense of humor. He blessed us all, including the American newspapermen who were traveling with us, most of whom were not Catholics. He assured them that it was just a little blessing and wouldn't do them any harm.

21

Early on the morning of February 22 we left Rome and flew to Berlin. From there we stopped in Bonn and then went on to The Hague. We had a delightful visit with the Queen of the Netherlands but came up against a number of Dutch leaders who were as intransigent in their position regarding West New Guinea as were some of their opposite numbers in Indonesia. The wife of a highly placed official told me that she had spent some time in Indonesia and in her judgment the Indonesian people still regarded the Queen of the Netherlands as their real ruler.

I had a stimulating meeting at the airport with some Dutch students. They were very articulate and extremely well informed and thoughtfully gave me a pair of wooden shoes for my son's birthday, which they had learned was that day.

From there we went on to Paris, where I met with General De Gaulle, and then flew back to the United States.

And so this, in outline, was our trip—which originated strangely enough as a result of a trip I made with the President to Tokyo in 1951. We had busy days and our time was continually occupied. Here is an example of a typical day's schedule in Japan:

A.M.
6:15   Attend Aikido Judo Exhibition.
6:30   Skating at Korakuen Ice Palace with workers of the Riken Kogaku Company and students.
8:15   Bus trip through Kawasaki industrial area of Tokyo. Visits to the following plants:
        Sony. Meeting with workers in the plant's auditorium.
        Nippon Steel & Tube. Meeting with workers and tour of the rolling mill.
        Fuji Denki. Tour of two main plants followed by question-and-answer period with workers in the factory mess.

P.M.
12:30   Press Club luncheon and speech.
2:30   Meeting with labor union representatives of Sohyo and Churitsu Roren unions.

3:30	Meeting with labor union representatives of Zenro and Shinsambetsu unions.
4:20	Call at U.S. Embassy annex to visit consular section and meet briefly with American and local employees.
4:30	Meeting with "R.K. Committee" Executive Committee members to discuss impressions of the visit.
6:00	Reception at the Japan Institute of Foreign Affairs offered by Dr. Gunji Hosono.
8:00	Dinner by the "R.K. Committee."
9:30	Calls at *Sankei, Mainichi* and *Asahi* newspaper plants to meet with editors and talk to workers.
11:00	Meeting with the American press.

And this schedule, as printed, does not tell the full story by any means. For example, on this particular morning before breakfast we were off to the Aikido exhibition to see how Japanese are trained in this wrestling art. Two members of our party, Hank Suydam, the *Life* Magazine correspondent, and John Seigenthaler, my administrative assistant, were invited to actively participate and were thrown head over heels and pinned to the mat by the instructors—who were only half their size.

Both John and Hank said they could have done better had they not been asked to perform on an empty stomach—but neither offered to come back and redeem his honor after eating.

From this demonstration we went directly to a skating rink where several hundred factory workers were enjoying a morning outing on the ice. Their reception was very warm. In fact the only thing cold about our stay was the temperature of the ice—which I tested at one point by falling on it.

As our trip proceeded from country to country I was struck by certain profound differences that marked these nations. For example, the press in Japan is a vast, complex and free enterprise which saturates the entire nation with news. Its reporters are competitive and industrious men and women and there are more photographers per square inch in Japan than anywhere else in the world. On the other hand, the press in Indonesia makes little impact. It is an arm of the government. It has no wide circulation and there was never a

23

problem in that country of being harassed by Indonesian
newsmen. In fact, during the whole trip through Indonesia
I don't believe I was ever questioned by an Indonesian news-
man, despite many opportunities for them to do so.

The difference in educational standards between these two
countries was also striking. In Japan the population is 99
percent literate. There are 700,000 students in college. By
contrast, when Indonesia's President Sukarno took over the
country from the Dutch, only a few hundred students attended college. There are now approximately 75,000. The
literacy rate has improved, but it still is only slightly over
50 percent. In Indonesia the influence of youth is beginning
to be felt, but in Japan the older generation still holds the
reins. Japan had the largest percentage gain of gross national
product in the world last year. In Indonesia the gross
national product might very well be moving down, if it is
moving at all.

There were even more obvious contrasts: In Japan and in
Berlin there is political democracy; in Indonesia a benevolent
dictatorship; in the Netherlands and Thailand a monarchy
supported—again in different ways—by a parliamentary system.

Yet in all these countries I was asked the same questions
again and again concerning the United States. A question
about the race issue was inevitable everywhere. In some
places where our plane stopped only to refuel, foreign newsmen would bring it up. I remember that Carlos Romulo, the
great statesman and friend of the United States, came to see
me just before he returned to the Philippines. He said that
unless we in America could find the answer to the racial
question and unless we made positive progress we could not
expect or hope to win the struggle with Communism.
Romulo said racial inequalities in the United States make
parts of our Constitution and our Declaration meaningless
to many. I believe this to be true. Whenever the question
arose, I made it clear that we were making progress in the
United States and I cited examples.

In every country I found a common strain of friendship
for the United States. There were pickets and minor incidents and small misunderstandings in some countries but
generally there was a tremendous undercurrent of goodwill.
Wherever I went I met free men who want to remain free

and who look to the United States for hope in the future.

In Berlin, for example, I met a couple of young students studying at the Free University of Berlin. Periodically they and some of their fellow students traveled to East Berlin to smuggle out relatives and friends from the Communist sector. They are the modern-day Scarlet Pimpernels. Just talking to them, and, in fact, traveling through Berlin for those forty-two hours, made me realize that this is a struggle which we cannot and will not lose. I reflected later on the plane that these people, young and old, who have risked death to find freedom in West Berlin are the wave of the future. To them, we in the United States have a special obligation, with them a special bond.

I remember that Ambassador Reischauer, when he encouraged me to make this trip, said the great problem we face in Japan is the growing feeling that the United States is a tired old country and that Communism and the Communists are developing young leaders for the future.

As the President pointed out, a new generation now carries the torch in the United States. "We must," as Ambassador Reischauer said, "try and project our true image around the world."

"Come to Japan," he told me. "You are young. You look rested. Come and offset this false feeling."

And so we went; we listened; we learned; we told people about the United States and about the American people. We left the United States, as Ambassador Reischauer said, young and rested. I'm not so sure we were in the same condition when we returned a month later.

In looking back on our trip I felt that personally I gained a great deal from my meetings with such respected leaders as Prime Minister Ikeda, President Sukarno, Chancellor Adenauer, Mayor Brandt, President De Gaulle and Prime Minister Sarit Thanarat. I was honored to have met such distinguished personages as the Queen of the Netherlands, the King and Queen of Thailand and, of course, Pope John.

But in the final analysis the greatest personal source of satisfaction came from the opportunity we had to meet and mingle with students, professors, labor leaders, factory workers, shopkeepers, silk weavers and others in each of these countries. If anything worthwhile came from this trip around the world—and I hope that it did—it is my belief that it grew out of exchanges and discussions and meetings with world leaders, of course, but, equally important, out of the informal, direct, challenging encounters with the people they govern.

CHAPTER 2

A Business Meeting

It has long been my impression from observing protocol in
Washington that very little that is of value comes from the
stilted formal receptions and dinners that are a part of official diplomacy. A visiting dignitary in Washington is honored at a reception and he stands in line with other dignitaries and shakes hands with hundreds of people he has no
opportunity to know or talk to. He goes to dinner and he is
seated between the wives of two government officials who
may—but probably don't—speak his language. These dinners
usually last several hours and are climaxed by a brief toast
addressed either to him or to his nation's leader and he eventually replies with a toast to his host or to his host's national
leader. For all practical purposes, there is little real chance at
either a formal reception or formal dinner to have direct
contact with people, to have any coherent exchange of ideas
and new thoughts, to find out about a country or its people
except through stiff and awkward dinner conversations. In
my opinion these affairs are largely a waste of time, although
they traditionally have been a part of diplomacy.

I hoped that functions of this sort could be held to a minimum on our trip abroad. In Japan I was especially fortunate
in this regard. As might have been anticipated, there was
originally a slight difference of opinion between government
officials and the citizens' group with which my old friend
Dr. Hosono was associated as to how our time would be
spent. Finally, it was determined that we would spend our
first day as guests of the Japanese Government, making the
necessary official calls, and the following five days we would
be the guests of the committee, devoting most of our time
to informal contacts with the people of Japan.

The meetings with Japanese officials were very useful.

27

They probably added little to international diplomacy and, in fact, they were not intended to. But I can't help feeling that it is most helpful for representatives of governments to talk openly about common problems face to face, rather than through stilted correspondence or cautious exchanges between intermediaries.

And so the first day in Japan I met Prime Minister Ikeda, Foreign Minister Kosaka, the speakers of both houses of the Diet, Chief Justice Yokota of the Supreme Court and Minister of Justice Ueki and his staff.

Before I left the United States I discussed with officials of the State Department the question of gifts for distinguished foreign hosts. They suggested such things as autographed copies of the President's books, ashtrays bearing the emblem of the Department of Justice, and—autographed pictures of me, in a frame bearing the Department of Justice seal.

I agreed with all those suggestions but the last. It did seem embarrassing to me to come to the end of a meeting with the Foreign Minister of Japan and then suddenly thrust on him an autographed photograph of myself. I could imagine his sick smile as he opened it and said, "Just what I always wanted." But the State Department said this is what is done. We compromised finally by giving everyone who received the picture a second gift as well. (When I gave the picture to one of the ministers, I told him that at least it was a nice frame and that he could take my picture out and replace it with one of his wife. He laughed, slightly nervously, I thought, as if I had read his own thoughts.)

Prime Minister Ikeda, an extremely attractive and able leader, was the first government official to receive me. He invited me to his home early on the morning after my arrival. He was dressed in traditional Japanese clothes and we removed our shoes as we entered his house. We sat cross-legged on his floor, sipped tea and had a frank conversation about our mutual problems. From the outset he made clear his strong friendship for the United States, but he did not hesitate to speak directly about such questions as trade and Okinawa and other matters where the viewpoints of our two countries are quite different. And the matters that we discussed that day were brought up again and again by every group with whom I met during the period of the next five days.

Japan purchased $1.74 billion worth of goods from the United States in 1961 and the United States purchased only $1.1 billion worth from Japan. Why were we considering raising our tariff barriers?

Japan bought $220 million worth of cotton from the United States and sold only $70 million of cotton textiles to our country. Why were we considering imposing new restrictions on these goods?

Why didn't we restore more civil rights to the people of Okinawa?

Why couldn't Japan have a larger role in the control over that area?

These subjects, in different forms, in different words, plus the inevitable question of nuclear testing, were continuously raised, from the first day in Japan to the last.

I think it is important that American officials visit abroad. But every representative of the United States Government who travels to a nation—whether it be friendly or unfriendly—should make every effort to acquaint himself with the broad range of problems that confronts the nation he is visiting. We in the United States have answers for their questions, which are perhaps not always completely satisfactory to them, but at least they represent a legitimate and understandable point of view. But I found we have not made our position clear in a forceful way, partly because many of those who have gone abroad did not know the answers themselves. And while, out of courtesy, some government officials of foreign countries may not press for answers, the people of these nations want and expect and, in fact, should have our position lucidly explained. From government officials and from the people in the streets I asked a free exchange of points of view. I received exactly that. And that was what was so helpful.

While visiting the Japanese Ministry of Justice I found lawyers and staffmen who were very familiar with our system of justice at every level. For example, an attorney who was escorting us through the ministry's various offices was explaining his country's judicial structure, and when he came to the bottom of the list he spoke of the magistrates who tried lesser misdemeanors.

"That is just like your J.P. courts," he said, in Japanese— but using English for "J.P. courts." He had been in the

United States some years before and had made a study of
our system. He was not, it should be added, impressed with
this aspect of our court system.

In the high-ceilinged reception room of his department
building, Justice Minister Ueki introduced me to his staff.
There were approximately forty of them, a far larger group
than its U.S. counterpart, but in many ways their duties corresponded to the responsibilities of the U.S. Department of
Justice staff. We all sat down for an informal discussion of
our departments. They had a tremendous interest in the
problem of Communist infiltration of various groups and
organizations in this country. Although the riots that prevented President Eisenhower from coming to Japan had occurred two years before, the violence and chaos were still
fresh in their minds. We talked about what had been done
in the United States to deal with subversion and to control
the spread of internal Communism, particularly as far as organized labor and youth organizations were concerned.

I explained that Communism had no broad appeal to either
group in the United States. I told them in some detail of
the work of the FBI and how, at a very early date, J. Edgar
Hoover had recognized the menace of internal subversion
and had taken steps to deal with it. I told them the story of
how the Communists during the 1930's had infiltrated the
American labor movement—and of how they were routed
from the inside by the leaders and members of the unions.

I described how James Carey waged war on the Communists who had taken over the Electrical Workers and beat
them; I related how Walter Reuther overcame, first the
Communist elements, and later the racketeers who tried to
take over the United Automobile Workers. I told them of
the leadership George Meany had given to this effort.

This was American history that seemed new to them. The
fact that citizens, banding together, with vigor, courage and
determination, had won the struggle against Communist elements made an impression.

I am well aware that what was possible in the United
States for our own labor organizations may not be feasible
in another country. But certainly part of our success in the
United States in controlling the spread of internal Communism has been due to the farsightedness of the FBI and to

the fact that organized labor in particular has pursued democratic, not Communistic, aims. Had Meany, Carey and Reuther and hundreds of other labor leaders and union members lost their fights in the 1930's, the situation in our country would be far different today.

The Minister of Justice in Japan, in addition to many duties which are similar to my own, also has responsibility for traffic safety. The automobile death rate in his country, especially in Tokyo, is very high. He asked for my advice on this subject.

I explained that this was a local matter in the United States and for him I had no suggestions—only sympathy.

We were welcomed to the Supreme Court of Japan by Chief Justice Yokota, the elderly jurist whose every action and word indicated a deep love of the law which has been his life. He escorted us to the chamber of the high court where the last word on Japanese law is spoken. Three walls of this grand room were covered with huge murals, each one depicting Japanese royalty in roles reflecting the three virtues considered essential to all judges in Japan: wisdom, benevolence and courage.

An antique lectern stands in the center of the courtroom, and from behind this lectern attorneys present their arguments to the chief justice and his fourteen colleagues. I walked behind the bench and noted that there was no gavel on the desks of the justices.

"There is no need for that here," Justice Yokota explained. "Our lawyers are honored to stand in this court. We don't need a gavel to remind them."

A short time later we visited the houses of the Japanese Diet—or Congress. I was accompanied on my visit to the upper house by Mr. Tsuruhei Matsuno, who began his service with that body forty-two years ago, or, as I told him, seven years before I was born. He invited me, while visiting his chamber, to sit in his seat and rap his gavel on the desk. The sound echoed through the empty chamber. I told him that I had seen no gavel in the Supreme Court and took this to indicate a slight difference in Japanese attorneys and U.S. lawyers.

He smiled and answered wisely: "Politicians are the same the world over."

31

The citizens' welcoming committee I mentioned earlier as having a hand in making plans for our stay in Japan was called the Young People's Committee for Better International Understanding. Organized with the help of Dr. Hosono (who, incidentally, is in his seventies), it gave itself the nickname the "R.K. (Robert Kennedy) Committee" for the duration of our stay, and organized the extensive schedule which was to bring us into direct and intimate contact with the people of Japan.

By the time we arrived, about 150 people of widely differing professions from the three Japanese cities we were to visit were on the host committee. They set up headquarters in a downtown Tokyo hotel six weeks before our arrival. They wore small badges on their lapels identifying them as members. They were young in spirit, though some of them perhaps not in age—the average age of committee members was over forty-five. Mr. Yasuhiro Nakasone, the young political leader whom we grew to like and admire greatly, provided much of the incentive and leadership. Our hosts offered to pay our travel expenses, which we explained was not possible, but they still raised some eighteen million yen ($50,000) to pay for the incidental expenses in connection with our stay in Japan. Only a third of this amount was needed, and so they applied the rest of the money to scholarships for foreign students studying in Japan.

It was on the second day of our stay that the "R.K. Committee" took over and we began meeting the people of Japan and getting their thoughts. My first such contacts were in round-table discussions—first with a group of business leaders, then with the representatives of several political parties. These were conducted at International House—a modern, glass-walled building of small rooms and sliding doors—a place which encourages discussion groups and which is well suited for small meetings such as ours, but not at all designed to accommodate the large numbers of Japanese cameramen who now turned out wherever we went.

There were about eight to twelve men in each group I met with and we sat around a table, with the translating being handled by Sen Nishiyama from the American Embassy. His translation was simultaneous, which is particularly difficult with Japanese and English, but he was fantastically good. He made a major contribution to the effectiveness of the meetings, and in fact to our whole stay in Japan.

Each of these round-table sessions was scheduled to last for about an hour. We would meet with one group while another would assemble in an adjoining room. After one discussion we would shake hands and I would walk through a sliding door into a second room and into the midst of another interesting exchange.

Some of the businessmen who took part in this first session were members of the "R.K. Committee," but this did not prevent them from speaking out. The business leaders—most of them in their forties and early fifties—took turns raising questions they had on their minds.

Mr. Tokusaburo Kosaka, the chairman of the "R.K. Committee" and the very able brother of the Foreign Minister, conducted the first meeting. He and his associates, one by one, stated their opinions and questions. At the end I was given an opportunity to sum up. Unfortunately, there was not sufficient time to answer all of the questions in complete detail. But many of their points were raised in later meetings and conversations.

Mr. Kosaka opened the meeting by discussing "strategy and tactics." He said the Soviet Union uses these devices to a better advantage than we do. He said he believed that military strategy dominated all of our thinking and that the Russians were cleverly beating us to the punch in non-military tactics.

The second speaker followed this up with a discussion of the Communists' cultural offensive on Japan, an extremely vital point, the importance of which was brought home to me again and again throughout our trip. He said, "The Bolshoi Ballet came from the Moscow Arts Theatre. Leningrad sent an orchestra. The Bolshoi Circus came. They sent, in addition to the ballet troupe, ballet instructors, and here now in Tokyo we have a ballet school that has been established with Soviet instructors participating.

"The cultural figures sent from the free nations are not very much different in number from the ones that are being sent from the Soviet bloc; however, in quality there is quite a difference.

"The Communists study very carefully to see what most

33

of the Japanese people want to see at a particular time. And then they plan very carefully.

"Now in the United States various organizations sponsor various cultural missions to Japan. But, in sponsoring them, the basic condition seems to be that it is done on a commercial basis. As a result, the admission fees to your cultural events are very high. The missions are not arranged on the basis of what the Japanese want to see, or on what the psychological and other conditions are at that particular time. As a result the effect of these American cultural missions has not been adequate.

"There are a number of groups growing inside Japan among the cultural intelligentsia—and they are effective and pro-Communist. For example, the Democratic Youth League in Japan is a growing front organization.

"Now the leaders of this organization don't set forth Communist objectives, but they start out purely on cultural and social activities to increase their membership.

"This organization is also tied in very closely with labor leaders from the group called the 'Ro-On,' which is a musical appreciation group of the workers numbering about 400,000, and also another labor group called the 'League of Worker Performers,' which has a membership of 100,000. This organized workers' force concentrates on bringing over cultural missions from the Communist bloc. They get the tickets out. The attendance at these performances is developed through these organizations. As a result of this the anti-Communist artists and performers here in Japan are finding it harder to make ends meet."

Another speaker went on to develop this point, and stated that the non-Communist efforts in the cultural field were insignificant compared with what the Communists were doing.

In later discussions it was possible to answer or comment on a point as it was raised. But with this group of businessmen, each of the participants spoke as he felt and there was no order or continuity in the matters they raised.

Later on in the session one speaker raised some significant points about the difficult problem of trade with Communist China. He said that the younger generation was being urged to stress trade with the free nations. Not only was it more economically advantageous to trade with the free countries, but it was realized that trade with Red China would lay

Japan open to Communist infiltration. Furthermore, trading with the Communists would antagonize the Free World, particularly the United States.

Nevertheless, he went on, China's needs and markets were expanding, and many Western nations were beginning to trade with the Chinese. "England is selling them trucks and other industrial equipment, France has made some agreements about exports with them, West Germany is already exporting to them, and Canada has agreed to sell them 45 million bushels of grain, including wheat. It is even rumored that the United States might sell some grain to them.

"The pressure on Japan to increase exports to the Chinese Communists is steadily growing. While the level of Japan's trade with China is presently still well below prewar levels, this pressure is a matter of grave concern to responsible Japanese, and the United States should be aware of this difficult situation."

Another speaker discussed the critical matter of trade from another angle. Why didn't we purchase more from Japan? Why did we have trade barriers to Japanese goods? What was Japan's future if the U.S. didn't welcome such purchases?

"Our economic situation still is not completely rehabilitated," this speaker said. "We are about to approach the stage where we will really be in a position to compete economically in the Free World. At present, 25 percent of our total exports are to the United States and 35 percent of our total imports are from the United States. This is evidence of the fact that we are not only dependent on the United States but that there is a dependency by the United States on Japan. So there is a mutual relationship between us.

"This problem is not only one of Japan's but also of the United States. And as long as the situation of trade between these two countries improves, why, the future will be optimistic, but if it deteriorates, then Japan may reconsider and will have to reorganize her trade setup."

Later on in the meeting, Noboru Gotoh, a leading Japanese industrialist, drew a unique analogy to characterize the relationship between Japan and the United States:

"Last year in autumn five members of the American Cabinet came to the Hakone conference, for a top-level conversation between our two countries. It was sort of a wedding ceremony—but the question I would like to ask is, 'Is this wedding going to be consummated?'

"With the presence of the Attorney General, I would just want to say, hold not only a wedding ceremony but a true consummation of the wedding."

I asked him what role he thought I should play.

"It is a vulgar way to say it, probably," Mr. Gotoh said, "but in Japan when two persons want to get to know each other—why, we may talk for a whole year, to get to know each other. And if we drink together, it will take us a month. But if we go out and play together, then we will get to know each other in a day.

"So that the visit this time here in Japan we hope will not be just one that is a put-on show, but one in which you will really get to know people.

"We take great pride in feeling that we are soldiers in the Free World camp, and every once in a while it is very painful to us when we find that we are occasionally ignored."

When this discussion ended I had the feeling that each man at the table with me was a friend of the United States. But each one had been honest and open in his questions about United States policy. They expressed themselves on matters that obviously puzzled and disturbed them. I had been concerned when I entered the room lest, because some of these men were my hosts in Japan, they would hold back their true views, but certainly this had not been the case.

I told them I thought it was probably impossible to try to discuss and answer fully each one of the points that had been made here and that that really was not my role. I was there to learn and was happy to hear what each of them had said and was grateful to them for speaking so frankly.

I said I thought the points that were made on cultural exchange were very helpful. This has been an area too much ignored by the United States.

"I would only point out," I said, "that there has been renewed emphasis on this over the period of the last year. Last week, for instance, we had some of our distinguished authors and educators here to make arrangements for continued exchanges between our poets and authors and artists and those active in music.

"The President personally is very much interested in this. This received its stimulus as far as Japan is concerned from the visit of your Prime Minister last year. We can expect that a good deal more can come out of this effort."

Then I went on to say, "In my meetings with your government officials yesterday, at no time did I say that, based on my visit, all the problems between Japan and the United States would disappear.

"An exchange in viewpoints is not really for the consummation of a marriage. What you say to me and what I say to you perhaps will help us understand each other better. It will insure that we have your viewpoint when we are making our decisions, and also that you have our viewpoint and our arguments when you are making your decisions. But it does not mean that our problems are going to disappear.

"If you feel that merely by sending our Cabinet members over, or by sending me, every difficulty between the United States and Japan should disappear, then it is ridiculous for me to come and it is ridiculous for everyone to come. Because that just cannot happen.

"A great deal has been accomplished in the United States in the way of understanding of Japanese position as a result of the recent visit of our Cabinet members. I was present in the Cabinet meeting when they reported to the President. They were extremely enthusiastic about the vitality and the vigor of the people and the educational standards here in Japan.

"I know from my own personal knowledge that following their visit the President spoke to a number of leading members of our Congress about the importance of continued trade relations with Japan. Those are significant results. But to expect that they are going to come here or that I am going to come here and suddenly the problems of trade between our two countries are going to disappear—that cannot be expected. What you are entitled to expect is that your position will be made known to the United States Government.

"We heard here today about the effect on young people if something should happen as far as trade relations with the United States are concerned—and that there would be a demand for you to turn to Communist China.

"But just put yourselves in the position of an American citizen. You have much cheaper labor here in Japan than we have in the United States, although you pay your labor more than any other country in Asia—and it continues to go up.

37

But you can sell your commodities at a lower price than Americans. So you export them to the United States.

"Well, hundreds, if not thousands, lose their jobs in my country because of that. We have four and a half million unemployed. Any action which puts numbers of our people out of work must be a matter of concern.

"On the other hand, you hear about the fact that England, France and Canada are selling things to China. We have a different position in my country. But we do not believe in a system of government where the most powerful nation tells every other nation what to do.

"We are not telling you. We are not telling England. We are not telling France.

"Now the Communist system is entirely different. They order others to do certain things. If their instructions are not followed—as happened in Albania and Yugoslavia—they are expelled.

"When we talk about strategy, our strategy is to get along with Japan. Our strategy is that the Japanese Government and the Japanese people should determine their own destiny, that they should not be dominated or controlled by any other power.

"That is not to say that in the course of our history, as Japan determines its own destiny and the United States determines its destiny, we won't have disagreements.

"I appreciate this opportunity to hear from you and to obtain your ideas. They will be reported back to the United States Government. I hope that out of this meeting will come a tolerance and an understanding on both sides for our mutual problems. That is what is important."

Following the session with Japanese business leaders, I was scheduled to meet with the representatives of three Japanese political parties.

Originally, I had expected to be able to sit down at the same table at the same time with all three groups. But this was not possible. Each of the three parties represents a distinct strain of political thought in Japan. Thus, three separate sessions were set up in three adjoining rooms. The Liberal Democratic party (LDP), the party in power and clearly the most influential group at the time of my visit, is extremely friendly to the philosophy of the United States. Its representatives raised the same questions about trade, nuclear tests and Okinawa that were on the lips of all Japanese. But they looked at these problems realistically. They accepted our point of view in the spirit it was offered. They were loyal to Japan, but they saw in this loyalty a need to protect freedom.

There were six members of the Diet in this group, including my friend Yasuhiro Nakasone, mentioned earlier. A bright, attractive and able political leader, I had first met him in Washington. He was one of Dr. Hosono's most persuasive emissaries in convincing me of the need for a trip to Japan and, now that I was here, worked hard to make our trip a success. But neither he nor his colleagues pulled their punches in our exchange of views.

The Democratic Socialists (DSP)—not to be confused with the Japanese Socialist party (JSP)—espouse socialism as the answer to Japan's problems. But they were not unfriendly. They too raised honest questions about our position on many matters. They sought honest answers. Their minds were open, and we can expect no more than this. One of their group, Mr. Eiichi Nagasue, a Diet member, also served on the "R.K. Committee," and when we traveled across Japan to visit Osaka he accompanied us to his constituency. He and Nakasone, I later learned, are good friends although they are of rival political parties.

The Japanese Socialists (JSP) came to our discussion with an entirely different outlook from either of the other two groups. The JSP has long paralleled the Communist party line. Their minds were closed to any point I presented. They did not want to understand. Looking back on it, I feel they hoped to turn our meeting into a propaganda victory for the Communist line over democracy. There were five members of their party—some of whom had recently returned from Communist China, where they had joined in issuing a communiqué with the Red Chinese hosts blaming the problems of the world on the "imperalism of the United States." Their chief spokesman was Tomomi Narita, a member of the Diet. They wanted to talk about nuclear testing and Okinawa, but they made it clear from the outset that they knew the United States was in error. They did not want to know what our position was; they wanted to know why we were so stupidly clinging to our beliefs. Why did we not change our position and accept their viewpoints on all these matters?

39

The following abbreviated transcript of my exchanges with Narita and the other JSP representatives reflects what I feel was one of the most rewarding of all the meetings I participated in on our trip. It began in a very friendly manner:

MR. NARITA: "Is it as bad as this with the cameramen in the United States?"

MR. KENNEDY: "Yes. I would say, however, that we don't have as many cameras. I think there must be a camera for every one and a half persons in Japan."

QUESTION: "Attorney General Kennedy, I want to pay my heartiest respects to your effort to see all sorts of people here in Japan—all strata of society. I had a chance to hear a little bit of the tail end of your meeting with the financial leaders in the other room. At that particular time you were speaking to them and they were listening."

"It wasn't always that way in the other room?" I replied amidst laughter.

QUESTION: "We are of the opposition party so I hope you will hear some of the opposition views."

MR. KENNEDY: "I thought I heard them up there with the financial leaders."

QUESTION: "We're all young people here. I myself am approaching fifty, so I am one of the older ones in this group. But in order to open the road and start the ball rolling I want to say a few words. The other day you mentioned that Japan is a very vigorous nation and it's a great nation and that therefore it should *not* take on a neutralist policy. About seven or eight years ago, the American leaders and also the Japanese Conservative party were saying that Japan is a weak nation and therefore it *should* take a neutral policy."

MR. KENNEDY: "Well, wait a minute. So that we get everything correct—I didn't say that. I think that what Japan does should be determined by Japan and the Japanese people. I haven't gone beyond saying that."

QUESTION: "I understand this. Now we Japanese people, through the experience of the last war—and now with a new constitution—feel very strongly about the safety and the security of Japan. The only way it can be insured is for Japan to take a neutral policy. The neutral policy means specifically *not* to ally ourselves with any country militarily. And so in a specific area—in the Asian and Pacific area—the Japanese people are hoping that we have a nonnuclear zone; an area that is not armed in nuclear weapons. We understand that China and the Soviet Union both are agreeable to this. If the United States would agree with this, then the hopes of the Japanese for a nonnuclearized area would be insured. What would you think about this?"

MR. KENNEDY: "I am sure the United States would agree to it, too. The United States would be strongly in favor of that. You would want, I am sure, to make certain that the United States was not taking any steps secretly to build nuclear weapons. Therefore, you would want to insist on inspections, would you not?"

QUESTION: "Yes. Well, it would certainly come into the whole field of inspection and control."

MR. KENNEDY: "Now, would that include Communist China? Would that include Siberia? And Manchuria? You feel that it would be necessary to have some kind of inspection of the United States. And would you at the same time require the same inspection of these other areas?"

QUESTION: "Well, the first thing, I believe, would be to establish this kind of a system. And then the inspection controls should come afterward."

MR. KENNEDY: "Would you think that was an essential part —the inspection? [Narita nodded affirmatively.] Yes. Well, then, could you, as their friends, make arrangements so that there could be some inspection of Communist China?"

QUESTION: "I think that control is a secondary problem. The establishment of the system comes first. Not to come to agreement over the question of control is the wrong approach."

MR. KENNEDY: "I would say—so that we understand each other right from the beginning—that you would have the United States in full agreement with such a nonnuclear operation in the Pacific—not only for the manufacture of atomic weapons, but the transfer of any atomic weapons and for the testing of atomic weapons. All of these things, as you say, in principle the United States would agree with completely. And we would sign such an agreement gladly. As you said at the beginning, however, inspection and control would be an important aspect of such an agreement. There must be some kind of inspection. We would be delighted to have representatives come through the United States or go through the Pacific. Now you just returned from Communist China. Could you give us some guarantee that Communist China would make such an arrangement also? How about northern Siberia?"

MR. NARITA: "Well, of course, Communist China still does not have such weapons at this point."

MR. KENNEDY: "How about Siberia? And Northern Manchuria?"

QUESTION: "In this whole question of nuclear testing and inspection there are negotiations going on between the Soviet Union and the United States. There are differences of views probably."

MR. KENNEDY: "Can I just say that this is a matter that really must be faced up to by you gentlemen. To preach generally that you are for an agreement and then ignore completely inspection and control frankly is not facing the facts yourselves, as the leaders of the Socialist party, or for your membership."

ANOTHER SPEAKER: "In relation to this thing, I would like to ask about what Mr. Narita was pointing out. As I understand it, there is a basic agreement on the principle of the creation of a denuclearized zone in the Pacific or in Asia. But we have recently heard that President Kennedy is faced with a decision about some conclusions he must make about atmospheric tests of nuclear weapons. We hear that probably atmospheric tests will be resumed. We Japanese—a country which first experienced the atomic bomb—cannot stand the results or the damages from tests that are carried out by either the Soviet Union or the United States. The United States starts up nuclear tests just because the Soviet Union starts up tests. You mentioned there is a basic agreement of principle. But before such agreement we want America to actually present practical actions in evidence of this."

MR. KENNEDY: "Can I answer that?

"We carried on negotiations for three years at Geneva—and voluntarily we did not test. In 1946, only the United States had the bomb. We offered to the Soviet Union at that time to ban the bomb—to ban the manufacture of it. You talk about China's not having the bomb. The inspection and control system we have suggested would eliminate the transfer of any weapons from one country to another. I would think that you people, having suffered as Japan has, would completely support the position of the United States in this matter. You can come over to inspect. You can walk through the United States. You can find out exactly what we are doing. We are an open society. Why aren't you critical of the fact that you can't do that in China? You can't do that in Russia. As Socialists who believe in the welfare of man and who are dedicated to the welfare of your own country, I cannot understand why you have not come out completely in support of our position, which would end the atomic bomb and testing."

SAME SPEAKER: "That is why we are saying that a great power like America must put this into practice in specific ways. The reports that we are getting about the resumption of nuclear tests is something we want to have stopped. Then the Japanese will support the Americans and Japanese thinking will change."

MR. KENNEDY: "Of course, the problem is that we sat down and conducted negotiations and voluntarily ended tests for three years: President Kennedy came into office and we went back to the conference table. While we were conducting these negotiations, the Soviet Union was planning tests. Now what can possibly be your answer to that?"

SPEAKER: So we also will be saying the same thing toward the Soviet Union and also toward China."

MR. KENNEDY: "I would be interested in that. Did you put out a statement in China criticizing the Soviet Union for resuming the tests?"

SPEAKER: "During the time of our discussions in China, I told them that we are opposed to any form of nuclear testing."

MR. KENNEDY: "Did you put a statement out criticizing the Soviet Union? I know you criticized the United States, but did you put out a statement criticizing the Soviet Union for resuming the tests? Did you say then that you are against this?"

SPEAKER: "We put out a statement in the form of opposition to all kinds of military action."

MR. KENNEDY: "You criticized the United States particularly and specifically. Did you criticize the Soviet Union for resuming the tests?"

SPEAKER: "Not in the words of a statement. As far as nuclear weapons are concerned, we did not one-sidedly criticize the United States in the statement."

MR. KENNEDY: "We hadn't just tested—how could you?"

QUESTION: "We also said in China we are against any kind of test. We are opposed to Soviet tests. The Socialist party position is that we are against nuclear tests in the Soviet Union, and this should be clear to them.

"Time is short. In order to deepen friendly relations between our two individual countries, an outstanding problem is that of Okinawa. From military necessity the United States still does not want to let go of Okinawa and return it to Japan. I think this is one of the basic causes of preventing further development of friendly relations between our two countries. The Chinese constantly attack us on the point that we are continuing to have the Americans on Okinawa. Why is it that the Americans are unwilling to return Okinawa to Japan quickly and remove the military bases there? This is something that we find intolerable—particularly our countrymen in Okinawa—they were particularly damaged during the war. A number of years after the war they are still under the control of a foreign nation. I think you should be able to understand this situation." [It is interesting that when this group criticizes the U.S. on Okinawa, they forget, conveniently, the fact that the Russians occupy certain of Japan's northern islands.*]

MR. KENNEDY: "I would say I understand that there were Japanese damaged during the war in Okinawa. I feel very badly about that. There were a number of Americans who were also damaged in Okinawa during the war. I feel badly about that, too. Since your Prime Minister came to the United States, the President of the United States sent a commission to Okinawa to study the situation there, to try to develop methods in which this matter can be improved. They have not yet made their report to the President. I would hope that we could make progress in this very important field. I understand your concern."

* Japan claims sovereignty over Habomai Island and Shikotan, now occupied by the U.S.S.R. While she does not claim jurisdiction over the Kuriles and southern Sakhalin, also occupied by the U.S.S.R., neither does she recognize the Soviet claim to sovereignty over these areas.

QUESTION: "As you know, the Socialist party wants to continue with this neutralist policy and we are not looking for or taking a position of animosity toward the United States. But in order to advance our position we must get this solution of the Okinawa situation.

"The other thing is the security treaty. To abolish this security treaty is the only way in which our true neutral position can be realized. The Conservative Government says that the security treaty with the United States has been established on an equal basis. I would like to ask whether this treaty can be abrogated any time that the Japanese side wants to abrogate it. It is something that was pushed on the Japanese. If the Japanese want it abrogated, would you be willing to abrogate it?"

MR. KENNEDY: "I don't think treaties are ever made with that viewpoint. I think they are made with the understanding that the terms should be lived up to, and as you depend on a person's word, you also depend on a country's word.

"It is a question of the country's word or the country's honor. I don't think a country can make a treaty and feel the other side is going to abrogate it or make it of no effect. I am sure you wouldn't suggest that."

QUESTION: "Frankly speaking, there was a great deal of expectation of the Kennedy Administration, ourselves included. We were also for the Kennedy Administration, but now some of us are a bit disappointed."

At this point they rose to leave. I said to them: "Wait a minute. I have something to say. I wish I had known of your support. We needed every vote possible."

I continued: "You have a Communist party here in Japan, is that right? And you are the Socialist party. Do you feel —and could I get a brief answer—do you feel that the Socialist party, your party, the Socialist party, could exist in a system in which the Communist party was in control? Do you feel that you could have these kind of discussions with a Yankee imperialist like me?"

They smiled and admitted: "No, we couldn't do that. But as a preface, such a Communist party wouldn't be able to take over in Japan, because we are here, the Socialists."

They again started to leave.

And again I stopped them.

"Wait a minute. I want to finish now. Can you answer another question? You have been critical of the United States. I gather, to say the least, that you don't think the United States is absolutely perfect. Except for the nuclear tests resumed by the Soviet Union, could you give me just three examples in the last two years where you have been critical of the Soviet Union publicly?"

There followed a considerable delay and consultation among themselves.

SPEAKER: "The only one is the nuclear test. In relation to our territorial problems we announced that some of those northern islands were Japanese. We publicized this. In the arguments about how to establish socialism in a country, we have had a great deal of criticism about them."

MR. KENNEDY: "Well, now—so we get a simple answer, can you give me three examples of where you have been publicly critical of the Soviet Union?"

(Again conversation lapsed and they consulted in whispers.)

SPEAKER: "The only one that I can recall is the nuclear test."

MR. KENNEDY: "I, for one, would say that that is of some significance.

"Shall I tell you what my impression is from our discussion? I appreciate your frankness. And I think you would expect the same frankness from me. And you are going to get it. I have been here an hour with you. You are the representatives of the Socialist party. Yet not one time have you brought up anything in connection with domestic affairs. You have not evidenced any interest in what we are doing in the United States in the field of providing a better life for our citizens. The fact that we raised the minimum wage to $1.25 an hour [again they got up to leave]—wait a minute —that we extended the coverage of minimum wage to five million more people; that we extended Social Security; that we passed the biggest housing bill that has ever been passed in the history of the United States; our efforts on education, so far largely unsuccessful, but efforts that have been made by the Administration; what we have done on civil rights —you haven't mentioned these things.

"We make mistakes in the United States and we will continue to make them. It is a government that is run by human beings and human beings make errors. But we are trying to do what is best for the people of our country.

"The people of Salt Lake City, Utah, or Des Moines, Iowa, or New York City just want to live in peace. And this government and this Administration wants to live in peace. We believe that every country and every people should determine their own destiny.

"Since the days of our revolution, through Thomas Jefferson, through the Civil War, to Franklin Roosevelt and Truman, to President Kennedy at the present time, the important thing for all of us is the importance and the dignity of the individual. The state exists for the individual, not the individual for the state.

"We believe that every country and every people should determine what is best for them. That is all that we ask. We are not attempting to impose our will on any other people. But we don't want an outside country to be determining the future of free people.

"So that is really what the struggle is all about. That is why, in my judgment, socialists throughout the world have been aligned with our system. I might say this: The most bitter opponents of the Communist system throughout the world—except for the Socialist party in Japan—have been the socialists.

"I would just like to have you analyze in your own lives and in your own teachings whether you are applying yourselves to work for the betterment of the individual Japanese [again they started to leave]—wait a minute. You spoke to me. I am speaking to you. Are you working to raise wages, to increase their medical care, to improve education? Rather than just criticize us—"

MR. NARITA: "The Socialists are the one party that actually insists on this strongly. It is true that on the surface the socialists and the Free World are against Communism, but just speaking about anti-Communism does not necessarily mean real anti-Communism. We can understand the American Government making a great deal of effort—"

I saw that he was ready to launch into a lengthy speech. I suggested that, as both of us had said our piece, we each take one minute to sum up and that we then end the session.

He hesitated and I got up to leave. I wished them good

luck and added: "Have some tolerance and understanding of the United States. We don't all have horns."

MR. NARITA: "We hope also that you will have some understanding, adequate understanding, about the Socialists. We would like to talk in the future, together. We are not just going along with the Communists, as the Conservative party maintains."

MR. KENNEDY: "After this visit I am going to watch very carefully for your public statements, not only to determine how we can improve in the United States, as I am sure you will be telling us, but what you are saying critically about the Soviet Union and Communist China."

I have serious doubts that anything I said made much of an impression on Mr. Narita and his friends. But it had some impact on the rest of Japan as the newspapers featured the fact that the JSP were asked for instances of criticism of the Soviet Union or China and that their answer was completely ineffective.

I later learned that while we were talking to the JSP leaders, members of the rival Democratic Socialists (DSP) were in an adjoining room. At times our voices rose, and I understand that Mr. Nagasue and his associates overheard much of the exchange and were delighted because they felt their rivals made such an unreasonable presentation. It made their own approach to such problems more popular, they felt.

CHAPTER 3

A Student Exchange

Most of the disorder and turmoil which erupted in Tokyo at the time of the Hagerty visit was stimulated by students and youth groups, which organized and led the chanting, screaming, snake-dancing mobs of anti-American demonstrators in 1960. Almost from the moment we arrived in Japan, we began to hear reports, some vague and others more specific, that demonstrations were being planned and that the Zengakuren (the leftist youth group held largely responsible for whipping up the frenzy of the demonstrations two years ago) were active.

Looking back on our week in Japan, I have no doubt that the Communist organizations were at work behind the scenes. But they failed to develop anything close to a successful demonstration at every point except one, Waseda University. Even at Waseda the vast majority of the students were either friendly or had an open mind and wanted to hear a representative of the American Government, and they eventually prevailed against those who sought to disrupt the meeting.

True enough, along the route I traveled in Japan, not only in Tokyo, but in Kyoto and Osaka, there were pickets carrying anti-American signs and chanting a chorus: "Kennedy, go home," "Go home, Bobby." They were few in number, however, and on several occasions we recognized the same pickets holding identical signs at different stops.

At one steel plant we visited in Tokyo, we were cautioned that there would be trouble, perhaps violence, and we considered canceling the stop. At the time of James Hagerty's visit approximately one thousand workers at this plant had left their jobs and rushed to the airport a mile away to join the group that threatened his safety. Nevertheless, we decided to go ahead with the visit.

When we arrived at the plant, twelve or fifteen pickets waited outside the gate with their familiar signs: "Kenedy stop oppresing Cuba." (It is interesting to note that the same misspelling of "Kennedy" and "oppressing" turned up on signs at almost every place we visited.) But inside the steel plant we were met with nothing but friendliness. As we toured the premises, workers gathered around in groups to shake hands, and we exchanged information about labor operations in our respective countries—how union officials are elected, who can run for office, how much they are paid, seniority, wage scales and so on. I felt the stop was most valuable, not only because these people were kind to me as a person, but because their interest and their questions clearly indicated a genuine feeling of friendship for the United States, and by implication regret over the incidents which had prevented President Eisenhower from coming to Japan. As much as any event in my trip it showed the shift in viewpoint over the past two years. I feel the change is due to a widespread counterreaction that set in following the riots and also to the hard and able work of Ambassador and Mrs. Reischauer, whose efforts have made a major difference. The results of their work demonstrate what just a few dedicated people can accomplish. Edwin Reischauer is a remarkable man; probably our leading foreign expert on Japan, he and his Japanese wife have won the confidence and friendship of many Japanese.

My first direct encounter with Japanese students was at Nihon University on the afternoon of my second day in Japan. Afterward we were to drive directly to Waseda University for another meeting with students—a meeting which was to be more informal than the Nihon appearance. As it turned out, this was quite an understatement.

Nihon University is the third largest institution of higher learning in Japan. I received an honorary degree of Doctor of Laws and then spoke in a huge arena-type auditorium which seats ten thousand and was filled to overflowing. There were no heating facilities in the building but the university officials made arrangements to keep at least one part of us warm by placing electric cushions on our chairs. This can be slightly disconcerting, especially if it feels too warm and you can't find the switch to turn it off. A text of my talk had been translated for the students and distributed to them. A huge screen was placed behind me and page numbers were flashed on the white canvas in order to help the students in following the speech. It was somewhat confusing to hear ten thousand people turn the pages simultaneously, and frequently the applause came at an inappropriate time in the middle of a paragraph. They realized as well as I did what was happening, so after several laughs at obviously misplaced applause we all settled down to do the best we could.

Actually, the first laughter came when I opened my remarks with a few sentences in Japanese. The audience thought I was speaking English and waited for the translation. Simultaneously we all realized what had happened and to everyone's relief I restarted in English. But they were all friendly and enthusiastic and there was not the slightest hint of anti-American feeling.

I felt it was important to make a number of points. In a more formal way I discussed some of the things I had mentioned in earlier encounters with the Japanese. I talked about our philosophy of government; that in a democratic system the state exists for the individual and not the individual for the state, and that the total effort of our system was to give our citizens a full life and yet protect our liberties and freedom. I said quite plainly that we do not try to impose our system of government on others but that we will defend our way of life "by affirmation, by argument and if necessary— and heaven forbid that it should become necessary—by arms.

"In accepting this degree I do so in the knowledge that you are doing more than honoring an individual. You also are signifying both curiosity and hope about my nation, my government and my political generation.

"I cannot expect fully to satisfy this curiosity and fulfill this hope but I can perhaps say something about the way in which my government—and some at least of my generation of Americans—look at the world. . . .

"Our generation was born during the turmoil following the First World War. . . . After 1914, the world as the West knew it began to go to pieces. The old certitudes started to crumble away. World War II came as even a greater disaster.

"Many young men, in my country as in yours, came

out of the misery and chaos determined to do everything they could to spare the world another such catastrophe —and to lay the foundation for peace and social progress. This determination committed them to a public career—in politics or in government service. The President thus began his public life by running for Congress in 1946. I was a student at college then, and my fellow classmates and I worked hard in that campaign. My brother went on to the United States Senate at the age of thirty-five, and when he was elected President of the United States, although to you and me he was quite old, he was still a comparatively young man of forty-three.

"In this the United States gave recognition to, and conferred responsibility upon, the generation which was born in the First World War and raised in the depression, which fought in the Second World War and launched its public career in the age of space. . . .

"This generation grew up in an age of instability and flux. From one viewpoint, this is the worst of times in which to live—a time of anxiety and doubt and danger. But from another viewpoint, it is a time of great stimulation and challenge. It is a time of motion, when society is cutting away from old moorings and entering new historic epochs.

"We in my country are by disposition and inheritance a people mistrustful of absolute doctrines and ideologies, persuaded that reason and experiment are the means by which free people fulfill their purposes. Yet we live in a century obsessed with ideology—a century that has been filled with leaders persuaded that they knew the secrets of history, that they were the possessors of absolute truth, and that all must do as they say—or perish.

"One of the great creative statesmen of our age was Franklin Roosevelt. He was creative precisely because he preferred experiment to ideology. He and the men of his time insisted that the resources of the democratic system were greater than many believed—that it was possible to work for economic security within a framework of freedom. . . .

"The turbulence of social change has long since begun to spill across national frontiers. The overriding development of the second half of the twentieth century is the awakening of peoples in Asia and Africa and Latin America—peoples stirring from centuries of stagnation, suppression and dependency. Now they are seeking through national independence the kind of economic and social development which both your country and mine have experienced. These are young nations, trying desperately in the quest for political and social progress to make up for lost centuries.

"The resources of the earth and the ingenuity of man can provide abundance for all—so long as we are prepared to recognize the diversity of mankind and the variety of ways in which peoples will seek national fulfillment. This is our vision of the world—diversity of states, each developing according to its own traditions and its own genius, each solving its economic and political problems in its own manner, and all bound together by a respect for the rights of others, by a loyalty to the world community and by a faith in the dignity and responsibility of man.

"We have no intention of trying to remake the world in our image, but we have no intention either of permitting any other state to remake the world in its image.

"In the unending battle between diversity and dogmatism, between tolerance and tyranny, let no one mistake the American position. We deeply believe that humanity is on the verge of an age of greatness, and we do not propose to let the possibilities of that greatness be overwhelmed by those who would lock us all into the narrow cavern of a dark and rigid system. We will defend our faith by affirmation, by argument and if necessary —and heaven forbid that it should become necessary— by arms. It is our willingness to die for our ideals that makes it possible for these ideals to live. . . . Freedom means not only the *opportunity* to know but the *will* to know. That *will* can make for understanding and tolerance, and ultimately friendship and peace."

I felt that the response of the students at Nihon to this address was indicative of the reservoir of goodwill that exists among the Japanese people for the United States. If there was a single anti-American voice raised among those more than ten thousand students, it could not be heard, nor would it have had the slightest effect on the warmth of the crowd in that cold arena.

We drove from Nihon to Waseda University. It never occurred to me not to visit Waseda, although this course was urged by some. Many of the students from this university had participated in the Hagerty disturbances. On the day of my appearance there were all sorts of stories about what the Communist students were planning for us. Their failure to drum up any real demonstration during our first day in Japan and the fact that they did not attempt to subvert the meeting at Nihon University made it seem reasonably clear that there was little chance that the Zengakuren could disrupt our stay in Japan. But the reports began coming in that they were going to make a real effort at Waseda.

Before I was to appear at Nihon and Waseda, Ambassador Reischauer and I discussed what we should do at Waseda should an incident occur. One account had it that pickets would lock arms and bar our way. Another version was that they would snake-dance around the auditorium building. Still another was that they would put shouting sections inside the auditorium and refuse to let the meeting take place.

We decided that should they attempt to prevent our entering the auditorium, the Ambassador and I would simply approach them and ask them to discuss in a reasonable manner whatever their complaint might be. If this should fail, we would continue along our way with an escort.

Looking back on my contacts with Communists at various stops on my trip, I am inclined to believe now that such an effort to talk would have been completely futile. The last thing any of these people want is reasonable discussion. Disorder, disruption, chaos, yes—an exchange of views and opinions, definitely no.

However, our plans were unnecessary because when we arrived at Waseda a crowd of some three thousand students or more met us and was entirely friendly. The only signs they carried said: "Welcome, Robert Kennedy," and "Hello, Bobby." My wife and I, accompanied by members of the citizens committee which sponsored our Tokyo visit, pushed through the throng of laughing, cheering students. They were boisterous and their efforts to shake hands and touch us were somewhat surprising in view of the ominous reports

54

we had received about the type of greeting that would await us.

These students had massed outside the Waseda auditorium to let us know they were our friends. Undoubtedly, they knew of the meetings the Zengakuren had held. Unquestionably, they had heard reports that we would be met by trouble. They wanted us to know we were welcome.

Inside the auditorium the story was different. There the Communist students made their only serious bid to spoil our trip. The building seated about 1,500, but 3,000 were jammed into the hall. They filled the aisles, the orchestra section, the balcony and spilled out into the corridors. Of this crowd of 3,000, only 100 or 150 participated in the efforts to wreck the meeting.

The students applauded as we entered and for a few seconds I had an opportunity to speak. (Mr. Nishiyama, whom I've mentioned earlier, once again did a simultaneous translation.) Then the disrupters, located strategically in twos and threes throughout the hall, many of them centered just in front of the stage, began to shout and jeer. Two members of the faculty tried to quiet the would-be riot-makers but their efforts were ignored by the Communists, some of whom we were told came from schools and universities other than Waseda. By tradition no law enforcement officers are allowed on Japanese campuses, and the school authorities seemed powerless.

One young man who made the most noise as I began to speak was located directly in front of the stage and slightly to my left. He was waving a leaflet which the Communists had distributed. At first I thought that if I ignored him he would subside. And so I began.

"My friends, I appreciate very much the welcome you have given to me and to my wife. We are here to discuss in a frank and candid manner questions which will be of interest to you.

"The great advantage of the system under which we live —you and I—is that we can exchange views and exchange ideas in a frank manner, with both of us benefiting. It is very possible that there are those here today who will disagree with what I say. [This was an understatement, to say the least.] But under a democracy we have a right to say what we think and we have the right to disagree. So if we can proceed in an orderly fashion, with you asking questions and me answering them, I am confident I will gain and that perhaps also you will understand a little better the positions of my country and its people."

The young man in the front row was still bellowing. To make matters worse, others who disagreed with him were shouting for silence and this added to the confusion. I decided to take another approach. I said: "There is a gentleman down in the front who evidently disagrees with me. If he will ask a single question, I will try to give an answer. That is the democratic way and the way we should proceed. He is asking a question and he is entitled to courtesy."

Later some school officials said they would have preferred it if I had continued to speak, rather than open the door to questions. But it would have been a waste of time. Already the bedlam was spreading. The Communists were yelling, "Kennedy, go home." The anti-Communists were yelling back, and the others were yelling for everyone to keep quiet. I could see I wasn't going to make any progress. It was at this point that I invited the young Communist with the loudest voice from his position in the front row, up to the platform to ask the question. He was dressed in a student's black uniform and my invitation obviously took him by surprise.

The rest of the students cheered and the invitation left him off balance for a moment. But once he was given an opportunity to ask a question, he seized the opening—and the microphone—and launched into an anti-American tirade which went on for five minutes, concentrating on our abandoning the traditions of our revolution and the occupation of Okinawa. At this point I asked whether he was going to ask a question or make a speech. This started him on an "exploration" into the democratic policies of the United States, ending once again on Okinawa. When he concluded, I took the microphone from him and began to answer.

Immediately every light in the house went out as the power failed—I could not believe by accident—and the microphone went dead.

For fifteen minutes there was complete chaos. I attempted to speak without a microphone. It was not possible. Everyone now began to yell—at me, at each other, at the school authorities. This only added to the confusion. Fortunately, however, one of the members of our party found a battery-operated bull horn in a storeroom under the stage platform and quickly brought it up to me. Ambassador Reischauer, who is well known and respected by the youth of Japan, moved to the front of the platform. He held up his arms and spoke to the students in Japanese. He was able to accomplish what none of the school authorities had been able to do. A quiet came over the crowd. Using a hand microphone, I succeeded in being heard.

"Let me just say this to you. Let me just tell you a little bit about what the United States stands for. Let me tell you a little bit about what we are trying to do in the United States. We were born and raised in revolution. We had many years in which to develop. We have been most fortunate. We believe in the principle that the government exists for the individual, and that the individual is not a tool of the state."

There was an outburst of applause, intermingled with shouts of "Kennedy, go home." I continued.

". . . We in America believe that we should have divergencies of views. We believe that everyone has the right to express himself. We believe that young people have the right to speak out and give their views and ideas. We believe that opposition is important. It's only through a discussion of issues and questions that my country can determine in what direction it should go.

"The future of Japan and the Japanese people should be decided by Japan and the Japanese people. Different viewpoints are expressed at this university and in our universities in my country.

"We are the heirs of the true Revolution. We are committed to progress while maintaining the rights and freedom of the individual.

"This is not true in many other countries. For instance, would it be possible for somebody in a Communist nation to get up and oppose the government of that country? . . .

"It wasn't necessary, for instance, for the United States to erect a wall to keep our people within our society as was done in East Berlin. If it's a workers' paradise on the other side, it is strange that it has finally come to this.

"I am visiting Japan to learn and find out from young people such as yourselves what your views are as far as Japan is concerned and as far as the future of the world is concerned.

"This world is in the hands of people like ourselves. Are we going to move forward or are we going to stand still? Are we going to accept what is the *status quo* or do we feel we can make progress? Are we going to improve the lives of our citizens and those in other countries that are less fortunate than we are? Are we? That is what the great struggle in the world is all about."

There was interest and some applause.

"President Kennedy believes there is an age of greatness before us. With all the perils that are facing us as young people, these challenges transform our life from a routine into a great adventure. We have ahead the new frontiers of science and technology and education. We want to move forward into these new frontiers. That is our philosophy."

I turned to the young man who had come to the stage and I continued: "This gentleman, who asked the question, said that we have abandoned our revolution—that we have gone backward rather than forward. I say the record proves otherwise."

Then I went on to talk about Okinawa, as I had to the Japanese Socialist party. I told them of the efforts that we were making and that improvements would be made.*

* On March 19, 1962, an amendment to Executive Order No. 10713 providing for the administration of the Ryukyu Islands was signed by the President. In addition, he directed that a number of specific actions be taken in order to express on the part of the U.S. a spirit of forbearance and understanding of the problems that exist in connection with these islands. These actions consisted of:

1. Asking the Congress to amend the Price Act (PL 86-629) to remove the present $6 million ceiling on assistance to the Ryukyu Islands.

2. Preparing for submission to the Congress plans for the support

There was a further limited exchange back and forth with the first student. He shouted that my answer was unsatisfactory. He wanted to make a further statement. I said I had come to listen to more than one student's opinion.

I could not avoid taking a special note of this young man. He had come forward under very difficult circumstances. He was tough, intelligent, intense and articulate. His frame was

of new programs in the Ryukyus to raise the levels of compensation for Ryukyuan employees of the U.S. forces and the Government of the Ryukyu Islands and the levels of public health, educational and welfare services so that over a period of years they reach those obtaining in comparable areas in Japan.

3. Preparing proposals for the Congress to provide over future years a steady increase in loan funds available for the development of the Ryukyuan economy.

4. Entering into discussions with the Government of Japan with a view to working out precise arrangements to implement a co-operative relationship between the United States and Japan in providing assistance to promote the welfare and well-being of the inhabitants of the Ryukyu Islands and their economic development, as discussed between Prime Minister Ikeda and myself during his visit to Washington last year.

5. Carrying on a continuous review of governmental functions in the Ryukyu Islands to determine when and under what circumstances additional functions that need not be reserved to the United States as administering authority can be delegated to the Government of the Ryukyu Islands.

6. Carrying on a continuous review of such controls as may be thought to limit unnecessarily the private freedoms of inhabitants of the Ryukyu Islands with a view to eliminating all controls which are not essential to the maintenance of the security of the United States military installations in the Ryukyus or of the islands themselves.

The Executive Order was designed to accomplish the following purposes:

1. Provide for nomination of the Chief Executive of the Government of the Ryukyu Islands by the legislature.

2. Restate the veto power of the High Commissioner, to emphasize its restricted purposes.

3. Lengthen the term of the legislature from two to three years.

4. Permit the legislature to alter the number and boundaries of election districts.

5. Provide that the Civil Administrator shall be a civilian.

6. Make certain technical changes in the provisions for criminal jurisdiction over certain Americans in the Ryukyus.

slight but his lungs were completely sound. He was filled with the Communist fire of dedication. He had accepted the party line, word for word, and he expressed it well and without question.

His face was taut and tense and filled with contempt. Those who in the next few days showed up at my meetings carrying signs and yelling displayed the same intensity, frequently with words and facial expressions of complete and absolute hatred.

A second student who came forward asked a question on Korea and why we were backing an undemocratic government there. His question was also lengthy. I explained in answer that the present Korean Government was instituting some necessary reforms after an era of corruption; that the United States had every expectation that following this period of transition the government would restore democratic processes. I asked for still other questions, and while many probably wanted to be heard, the fact that they had no microphone hampered communications.

Finally it was suggested we end the meeting, so I closed by saying:

"I don't think this is the easiest form in which to exchange ideas, but I appreciate your invitation and your courtesies to my wife and myself.

"I want to say just a personal word to all of you. My brother, the President, entered politics at a young age.

"Although now President, he is still young, and all those who held key positions in his campaign are young people. He believes that the future of the world belongs, not just to the younger generation of my country, but to the younger generation of all countries. We have a role to play—you and I. We have responsibilities and obligations to our own people, to our own country, but also to the people of the world. There has to be tolerance and understanding between all people. . . .

"I would say we are facing many of the same problems in the United States that you face in Japan. The solution for all of us is to join as brothers to meet these difficulties. There are great problems. There are great challenges. The age of greatness is before us and we, joined as brothers, can meet our responsibilities and obligations and make this world a better place for ourselves and for our children."

After I finished these remarks a young man equipped with even more powerful vocal cords than the Communist boy rose in the rear of the hall and began to bellow a statement. Because of the language barrier it was impossible for me to tell whether either the United States or I was being acclaimed or damned. The interpreter then told me he was the school cheerleader, and that he was expressing an apology for the student body. With that he came forward to lead the student body in the school song.

During the first chorus he accidentally struck my wife in the pit of the stomach. She said it didn't hurt, or at least not nearly so much as it would have if he hadn't been a friend. The song was a rousing one and on this note we left. As we walked across the back lawn to our waiting cars, Professor Nakatani, who had been in charge of arrangements, said he thought Japanese students still are too immature for such exchanges. But, he said, he was glad the student had been invited to speak out. "Something I am glad of," he said, "is that there was no violence."

He spoke too soon. The students were leaving the auditorium, too—but they broke all the chairs in the place on the way out.

Later in the week, the cheerleader, Shunji Nagasawa, came to the Embassy residence and we presented him with a copy of Carl Sandburg's book *Abraham Lincoln*. He was an exceptionally bright young man and I was happy to have him on our side. He was democracy's effective, quickwitted and tough answer to the Communists.

Live television cameras had covered the Waseda appearance. As we learned over the next few days in our trip around Japan, many, many people had watched the whole affair. Further, it was played in whole or in part on many of the evening television shows.

Some of our friends on the "R.K. Committee" feared at first that this wide coverage would hurt the effect of our visit—that many Japanese would take this to be the "Hagerty incident" all over again.

But other members of the "R.K. Committee" said the effect would be favorable. Yasuhiro Nakasone said that the gesture of giving a dissenter a chance to be heard would leave a favorable impression. Kazushige Hirasawa, the noted TV commentator and critic, with his wrinkled brow and gloomy manner, whom we came to think of as "the Edward R. Murrow of Japan," said the fact that the Communist efforts failed would bring about a reaction against the Communists and in favor of the United States.

He was correct. As the week wore on, overwhelming sentiment built up against the demonstrators. The *Asahi Shimbun*, Japan's largest daily, reported a record-breaking number of letters to the editor concerning the Waseda speech and the editorial pages reported 80 percent were favorable to the United States.

A few days later in Kyoto a boy wearing a student's uniform stepped from a crowd and asked me to autograph a copy of the President's book, *Profiles in Courage*. As I obliged he told me he was a former Waseda student. He said the entire country was disgraced by what had occurred. I told him I felt that everyone had a right to speak out and a right to be heard. Still later on my return to Tokyo I learned that a group of three hundred students from Waseda had come by to apologize. They had circulated petitions protesting the actions of the few and 2,200 had signed these petitions.

Actually, we were surprised at what an impact the incident caused. When we returned to the United States there were many groups of Japanese who came to my office to visit. Invariably, they brought up Waseda and almost inevitably they apologized for my treatment at the university. I explained that no apology was necessary, that no one had been hurt and that we had enjoyed the exchange. I think, however, that the reason the Waseda incident did make such an impression was that many Japanese, including university students, had become conscious of the fact that with democracy and freedom also must come discipline and maturity—that otherwise instead of democracy there will be anarchy and a dictatorship by either the extreme left or right.

CHAPTER 4

A Dialogue with Labor

The day after our return from the visits to Nihon and
Waseda universities, I met with another group for an informal session of give-and-take, arranged, as before, by the
"R.K. Committee." I had already had fruitful discussions
with representatives of the Japanese business community, and
with leaders of the major political parties. Now I had an opportunity to meet with representatives of the Japanese labor
movement.

The labor movement in Japan is a vital element. A total
of some nine million workers from a total labor force of 45
million have joined the ranks of organized labor. And that
figure is growing daily. There are three large national union
federations and several smaller groups.

The biggest is Sohyo (the General Council of Trade
Unions of Japan), which has about four million members.
This organization was established in 1950 as a protest against
the then leading union federation, Sanbetsu, which was controlled by the Japanese Communist party. Immediately after
Sohyo broke away, however, Sanbetsu quickly went out of
existence and much of its membership joined Sohyo. Today
the leadership of the union favors extreme left-wing socialism and its strength lies in membership among public service
workers, postal employees, railway workers, teachers and
municipal and prefectural employees.

Zenro (the Japan Trade Union Congress) is in turn an off-
shoot of Sohyo. It was established in 1954 by unionists who
bolted Sohyo, feeling it was leaning too far to the left. Zenro
has slightly more than one million members, most of whom
are textile workers, seamen and electricians. The organization is anti-Communist. While Sohyo gives general rank and

file backing to the Japan Socialist party (JSP), the Democratic Socialist party gets most of the backing of the Zenro members.

The third major union federation is Churitsu Roren (the Liaison Conference of Neutral Unions), which is a loose amalgamation of industrial worker groups, whose members number slightly under one million. Ideologically this organization stands closer to Sohyo than Zenro does, and its members, while maintaining their independence from Sohyo, sometimes do join that organization in protest demonstrations.

One of the more stimulating personalities I met on my entire trip was a labor leader named Akira Iwai, who represents Sohyo. In his early forties, he has an alert mind. I was much impressed with him as with other labor leaders, such as Minoru Takita, the president of Zenro. It is imperative that men like these know what we stand for.

In many ways Iwai was as confused about the American way of life—where we came from and where we are—as were some of the students we met in his country. Some of the obvious things about the United States, matters that we take for granted, seemed new to him. He is a forceful figure, but it appeared that he was learning about our system of government for the first time. He had sharp prejudices and he seemed never to have questioned his beliefs. It was an amazing experience for me to have such an able individual say, for instance, that the United States was run by the Morgan bank and really appear to believe it.

Iwai describes himself as a neutralist and a Marxist, though he declares that he is not a Communist, and yet some of his statements showed clearly that he had accepted the Communist propaganda about our way of life in the United States. Labor leaders in Japan—like labor leaders in the United States—are concerned about social and humanitarian developments and Iwai raised the question of nuclear testing soon after I sat down with him and five of his associates in Sohyo and Churitsu Roren. Why, he wanted to know, were we contemplating resumption of nuclear tests?

I replied: "The reason that testing will be resumed, if it is, is because the United States and the Free World will not be blackmailed into surrender by being weak."

I then went into the history of our experience with the

Soviet Union in the area of nuclear development, as I had with Narita and the other leaders of the JSP, and recounted our continuing efforts to secure a meaningful control over atomic weapons and testing. In view of the Soviet's breaking of the moratorium and resumption of testing in the summer of 1961, I said there was a strong possibility that we would have to resume testing.*

I then continued: "Our government and the American people feel this is the most important issue facing mankind; I can understand your own personal concern, having suffered in the war as you did.

"All I can say is that the greatest effort is being made in this area. Unfortunately, we do not live in a world in which we can just unilaterally disarm and expect to survive.

"This lesson was brought home to us in Geneva. While we were discussing in good faith, they were making plans for testing. If it happened once, it certainly can happen again.

"These atomic weapons can be transferred from one country to another. We want to prevent that—we want control—we want inspection.

"I would say that, in addition to the Soviet Union's having atomic weapons, Communist China is planning a nuclear capability. And if the United States either loses its weapons or loses its capability or strength, what happens to the people of the world? What happens to Japan? What happens to you?

"I would think that all that you would require of us is that we understand the implications; that we make the greatest human effort possible to reach such an agreement; but after we have made that effort, if we find that it is unsuccessful, that you support, in your minds, at least, our final decision, knowing what it means not just to the American people, but to the people of Japan."

Mr. Iwai said: "We certainly do not want to approach this problem from an unrealistic standpoint and purely from a so-called idealistic position. But at the same time, our feelings are that since we have experienced the atomic bombs and some of the dust from the first hydrogen bomb test, and things of this type, we do not want tests to be resumed.

"We still feel unsafe and concerned when the approach

* Testing was resumed on Wednesday, the 25th of April.

is taken that there has to be a balance of military power in the interest of peace. It appears to us as though this is more of a balance of threat than a matter of keeping the peace. And this is where we feel a deep sense of uncertainty. There is this increasing fear that one bomb can destroy so much, and these powers possess many, many of these bombs. They could actually destroy human civilization."

Mr. Iwai and his associates went on to raise questions they had on their minds about the treatment of the Communist party in the United States. He felt we were abusing "a legitimate political party." They had read about laws we had passed against internal subversion. They knew of the indictments the Department of Justice had returned against the Communist party shortly before I made this trip. They felt this was a form of persecution.

One of the labor leaders said that at a convention of Sohyo a resolution was passed opposing the Smith Act in the United States. He pointed out that most of the members of Sohyo are non-Communist.

Mr. Iwai said: "However, I feel to outlaw the Communists by this method brings up the question of whether it is the right thing to do. This is where I am doubtful. I prefer to see in the United States your correcting these situations about Communism through public opinion. That is the right way to do it. Just doing this by passing a law won't solve the problem. So I would ask the United States Congress and the United States Government to reconsider this. This is what I hope they do."

I asked Iwai if his people felt as strongly on the question as he did. He nodded affirmatively. I asked: "Is it their understanding that the Communist party in my country has been outlawed?"

Iwai replied: "I used the word 'outlawed.' I should have been more precise. Such things as the proposed fine of ten thousand dollars a day for delay and such things as these. These things I am aware of. In other words, the idea of using law to control or suppress."

(It was generally accepted in Japan and elsewhere that we had "outlawed" the Communist party. However, the fact that Iwai used that expression and then retreated from it, but knew about the penalty of $10,000 a day for failing to register, showed he was well informed on the subject.)

I explained that the Communist party was not "outlawed," that they could and did make speeches advocating their beliefs, publish newspapers, petition, assemble and all of the rest. I explained that any organization controlled and financed by a foreign power had to register with the Department of Justice, and that Congress passed legislation specifically to cover Communist compliance with that requirement.

MR. KENNEDY: "An act was passed in 1950, with the overwhelming support of the American people, defining the Communist party as a representative, not of American citizens, but as following the orders and instructions of the Soviet Union, and therefore a representative of a foreign power in the United States, and that it therefore should register.

"There is overwhelming evidence that that is true, and that the Communist party in the United States is financed by the Soviet Union. And I think that is true of most Communist parties in the world. They follow the leadership of the Soviet Union. They are not looking out for what is best for the Japanese people or the American people, but what the Soviet Union tells them. Let me give you an example of the 'party line' recently in my country.

"On the question of testing, the Communist party in the United States, through its newspaper, the *Daily Worker*, came out each week against testing. The week before the Soviet Union started testing, they wrote a very strong editorial against resuming nuclear explosions. Then the Soviet Union began their series of tests. The next week they came out for testing.

"Now, the question in our courts was whether the Communist party was an agent of the Soviet Union. And this was litigated back and forth in our courts for ten years.

"Every legal defense possible was available to the Communist party. The case went up to the Court of Appeals three times and to the Supreme Court twice, and finally the Supreme Court decided last summer, eight votes to one, that the Communist party was in fact dominated and controlled by the Soviet Union. A majority of the Court held that as a representative of a foreign power it should register with the Attorney General.

"Now this is the law of the land, upheld by the Supreme

Court. So if the representative of the British Broadcasting Company, which is owned by the British Government, refused to register, and after having been given notice, told the American Government that it was going to ignore the law, we would indict the British Broadcasting Company.

"The facts about the Communists were presented to a grand jury. And the grand jury of American citizens indicted the Communist party."

IWAI: "I don't want to argue about this problem, but in the case of the Japanese Communist party it is a fact that the Japanese Communist party also supported the Soviet nuclear tests. I don't think there is much difference in the viewpoint as far as things of that type are concerned. But the differences come from here on. It is not necessary for me to defend the Communist party, because I am not a Communist. The question is that the act itself requiring this kind of registration, requiring the Communists to register—is this the right human way to treat people in the truly democratic sense? Rather than for the courts to decide, I think the people should decide."

MR. KENNEDY: "The people have decided. You might disagree, and there is disagreement on this issue as there is on every issue in the United States. But the legislation and requirements are not so extreme as to horrify anyone. That is my point.

"And you might have a better way of dealing with the Communist party, but this is the way we have decided is the best for us. It is a fact that Americans resent that we have a group within our country who are taking orders from an outside power.

"You can advocate almost anything in the United States. We have groups that go around swallowing goldfish. People go around and say 'Heil Hitler!' That is a democracy."

These labor leaders were concerned—as was almost every sector of Japanese society—with the question of our role in Okinawa. Here, as before, I related their Prime Minister's discussions with President Kennedy and the resulting investigation of the situation.

They were equally interested in trade problems, primarily because if trade relations with the United States deteriorated it meant a difficult time for their union members.

I told them of the major effort the President was making

in the United States on the question of world trade. I said:

"He feels that it is so important that despite the fact that this is an election year, and this effort poses difficult political problems, he is making the effort now rather than waiting until 1963.

"He has recommended that we enter into these agreements with the Common Market in Europe, lowering trade barriers and tariffs on large numbers of goods.

"Under the most-favored-nation clause, these benefits will also go to Japan and other countries of the Free World. So that will be an important step forward.

"The President is very much aware of the fact that Japan buys more from the United States than it sells to the United States. Therefore, the purchases that Japan makes in the United States give jobs in my country. He feels that this point is not sufficiently known in the United States. He has discussed it at Cabinet meetings, and he has also brought it up with influential members of Congress.

"He understands that Japan has to trade in order to live; and markets other than the United States have to be opened to Japan. He has told the leadership of Western Europe that they and the United States cannot become economic fortresses within themselves. They cannot be two powerful blocs trading just with one another. Both areas have responsibilities to other nations—the more backward countries and those countries which have trade problems. He has made this quite clear.

"So the trend in the United States is to lower tariffs. We have immense problems in our country, too. We have four and a half million people who are unemployed.

"And the President is studying this, knowing our responsibility in this trade field; knowing how important it is for the survival of the Free World; knowing also how important it is that there be confidence in the dollar and that the United States have a thriving economy.

"I would say to you as a general matter that the trade barriers in the United States are going down, but on individual commodities I cannot say that there would not be some disagreement between Japan and the United States. I think that there has to be a mutual understanding and exchange of views, and in my judgment these matters can be worked out satisfactorily.

"Just let me give you one personal experience.

"I come from the State of Massachusetts. One of our chief products was textiles. Right after the war, virtually all of our textile mills left the cities of Lawrence, Fall River, New Bedford and Lowell, and went into the Southern part of the United States where wages were lower. We had tens of thousands of unemployed. Lawrence was a devastated area for five or six years and posed an immense problem.

"A major effort was made, led by the President, then as a Congressman and later as Senator, to bring new products into Massachusetts—electronic machinery as well as textiles. Now Massachusetts enjoys a generally healthy economic life.

"Therefore, the President is very well aware of the implications of this problem on all sides. He knows a good deal about it personally. He is conscious, not only of his responsibilities to the American people, but of his responsibilities to insure that Japan has a thriving economy, as a bastion of the Free World."

IWAI: "I can understand your situation after what you just now described, but at the same time Japan must increase her export trade. So we must exert efforts, too, in the direction of China and the Soviet Union, to parallel the efforts in the other countries. This I hope the United States will understand. England just sold some jets to Peking. They sold some agricultural machinery also. There is very little trade between China and Japan, but trade is going to be expanded. And I hope the Americans will understand the Japanese situation."

Business leaders with whom I had talked during my first day in Japan had raised the same question about nations of the Free World trading with Red China, pointing out that Japan's trade with the Communists was limited. But Mr. Iwai's attitude was noticeably different on this score from that of business leaders who had indicated a reluctance to expand trade with the Chinese. I suggested to Mr. Iwai that the question of Japanese trade with the Communists was one that would have to be decided by the Japanese.

He continued: "Do you have any questions for us, or any points of advice?"

I said that I had no advice, but I asked if labor organizations in Japan played a role in seeking the passage of social

legislation. Mr. Iwai said they did work through the Socialist party in an effort to get their aims passed into law. He
argued, however, that officials of the government in power
never consulted with representatives of organized labor on
questions of legislation. I pointed out that it was quite different in the United States. He said he was aware of this and
expressed appreciation for this meeting, which he claimed
could not have occurred with a Japanese official.

I then asked him about the communiqué that the socialists
with whom Sohyo is chiefly associated issued when visiting
Communist China, stating that the United States posed the
great menace to the world, that it was an imperialistic country. "Is that the belief that the labor movement has about
us?"

IWAI: "I need to explain the meaning of the word. The
word 'imperialism' is used in the sense of monopolistic capitalism. Ordinarily, imperialism has the meaning of something
where you take a whole bunch of troops and go in and take
over a country. In cases like Cuba or Laos, these things happen. We are not very well impressed with the way the Americans have been doing it in some areas. I don't mean that the
American troops landed in Cuba, but in general it appears
that they were trying to support or assist in this.

"We are using this term in the meaning that there is a big
monopolistic capital force in control."

KENNEDY: "You call the United States imperialistic. Based
on what happened in Tibet and Hungary, then do you consider the Soviet Union and China imperialistic?"

IWAI: "There were some mistakes made."

KENNEDY: "Do you consider them imperialistic?"

IWAI: "We don't use that term."

MR. KENNEDY: "Why do you use it for the United States
and not use it for them?"

IWAI: "Well, we determine it in the United States as mo-
nopoly capital."

MR. KENNEDY: "So I understand. It is permissible to send
troops in and kill people? Then one is not imperialist?

"I mean, honestly, you know that the United States, run
by this Administration, is not made up of a lot of monopolistic capitalists. Did you gather that from Arthur Goldberg,
who visited Japan some months ago and who came from the
Steelworkers Union? Or, for instance, from me? Or from a

country that raised the minimum wage to a dollar and a quarter an hour and passed all the other social legislation? Does that make us imperialists? Capitalistic imperialists?

"And the Soviet Union puts a wall up to keep their people in this workers' paradise, and they march into Hungary as they did, and you don't call them imperialists?

"As an amateur in diplomacy, it confuses me."

IWAI: "I am not making an issue of whether you come from a monopolistic capitalist country. Of course, the United States has shown some very good results in social security, housing and these things. But the basic characteristic of your nation is capitalism. Isn't that true? With Morgan, Rockefeller and all of these in control?"

KENNEDY: "You are talking about the United States a hundred years ago. Do you think we have stood still? And do you think the labor movement of the United States is run by capitalist imperialists? They are supporting President Kennedy. Walter Reuther—is he a capitalist? This is a different country now. This is not the kind of society that Marx was talking about a hundred years ago.

"Obviously, there were mistakes made, and there will be mistakes made in the future. But for groups around the world to mouth these ideas and phrases and slogans—it makes no sense. We are not run by the Rockefellers or the Morgan bank. I don't want to be facetious with you. I think that you have presented your position forcefully and reasonably. Obviously on some of these matters you have given a great deal of thought and you have great concern. For this I have great respect.

"But I ask that you examine the facts. Analyze what the United States is about. If you were to give us a fair shake, you would realize that this impression you have is not correct. Have you ever been to the United States?"

IWAI: "Yes."

KENNEDY: "Would you come again? Will you come again?"

IWAI: "Yes, I will eventually go *over* there."

KENNEDY: "How about coming this year? Come this spring. And you can see the United States and see who is running our country.

"Will you come this spring?"

IWAI: "I must go to Europe."

KENNEDY: "After you finish Europe, you can come to the United States?"

IWAI: "I don't want to argue with you, Mr. Attorney General. I recognize that capitalism has been changing. I don't believe that the capitalism that Adam Smith wrote about a hundred years ago is the capitalism of today. But I say that basically capitalism has not changed. There are many, many progressive areas, as you have said. We try to look at it fairly, as you have asked us to do. So we are not saying that we agree with everything that the Soviet Union and Communist China do—at least most of the Japanese trade union members don't.

"We observe socialism and at the same time make up our minds on the basis of the facts that are taking place. And so if the Soviet Union resumes tests, we oppose it strongly, as we brought out a while ago. We want you also to look at the Japanese trade union movement accurately."

KENNEDY: "I am trying to do that."

IWAI: "I thank you very much for your time."

KENNEDY: "Now, we are not forgetting this matter. I have learned a great deal visiting Japan. Thinking over the last few minutes of what you have said, I realize you have a complete misconception of what kind of government and what kind of people we are.

"We don't have child labor. We have Social Security. We try to educate our people. We have a minimum wage. We have working conditions that are desirable. And we appoint such fine men as Ambassador Reischauer to Japan. That is a pretty good combination.

"So you come to our country."

QUESTION: "Well, the thing that is good about this ambassador is that he listens to the opposition people, too. He is quite different from the previous ambassador."

KENNEDY: "You come to our country, now. I want you to meet some of our people. It is a good country."

We then met with a second group of labor officials from the Zenro and from a small neutral union group called the Shinsambetsu. There is tremendous competition between Zenro and Sohyo, as well as a completely different ideology. They refused to sit down together although many of their questions covered the same areas of interest: nuclear testing and trade, for example. The Zenro officials impressed me—

they were obviously responsible and hard-working and vitally interested in the welfare of their members. There was not the overtone of conflict with them that I felt with the Sohyo officials. Although they are dedicated anti-Communists, they were very outspoken on certain policy questions on which they differed from the United States.

Mr. Takita of Zenro expressed considerable concern about the corruption within the Teamsters Union. How had it happened? Why couldn't the members clean it out and what was going to be done about it in the future? I said these were matters that greatly disturbed the labor movement as well as the American people generally and that they were receiving our continued attention in the government.

Earlier on the day of my meetings with these labor officials, I had visited a milk-processing plant and a Zenro union member had raised an interesting and significant question on this whole subject of the future of the democratic system and labor management corruption.

"What happens," he said, "when a society becomes affluent? Do you lose your moral values?" I replied that certainly it did not have to be so. The United States, which had the world's highest standard of living, was made up of a citizenry exceptionally unselfish in its attitude toward its own people as well as other people of the world, and a governmental system which was dedicated to freedom as well as to the prosperity of its citizens.

I told Mr. Takita what his union member had said. We were both optimistic about the future but agreed that only time would give the full answer.

A true democracy, to survive, to prosper, must have a strong, dedicated, militant labor movement. Its leaders must be devoted to their members, to an ideal. In my judgment a labor movement is the backbone of a democracy. With the type of labor leaders that Japan possesses this is a tremendous potential for the future. The next three or four years will be critical, and their efforts need all the encouragement, through advice and example, that they can receive from the labor movement and others in this country and the other free nations of the world.

CHAPTER 5

The People Speak

Two days after Waseda, we traveled into other areas of Japan. At Kyoto a seven o'clock breakfast meeting was arranged with a group of labor leaders, followed by a conference with students from universities and colleges. The night we arrived our hotel was picketed by a group of Communist youth leaders. They marched up and down in front of the entrance and we could hear them calling out slogans as we made our way to our room (where, incidentally, we slept on the floor, Japanese style, which we greatly enjoyed).

The next morning, as we approached the small dining room where I was to see the young people, I was told that at a gathering the night before the members of the leftist organization had met and decided that their representatives could not attend the breakfast session; they should picket and yell slogans but should not talk. Eight other youngsters —all articulate and interesting and non-Communist—were on hand. They were student leaders not aligned with the Zengakuren.

As we entered the room and sat down to our meal of shrimp and seaweed, it was announced formally that the six Communists had decided to boycott the meeting.

"I am very sorry that they have not come," I said. "I don't bite. I think it is very important in a democracy to exchange views. It is the easiest thing in the world to denounce, or to make speeches from far off. If a person has facts to back up his position, in my judgment he should be willing to come in and discuss it. I don't think it is very courageous to denounce an individual or a group from a distance and not be willing to meet him face to face.

"That is my personal point of view. But I appreciate your coming."

A young student in a school uniform said the group was sorry that the six Communists would not attend, since their presence would have given me a more comprehensive view of the range of Japanese opinion. He went on to add:

"I am just a Japanese student. I am not an official representative of any group nor am I a Communist. With respect to the struggles that have been demonstrated against the security treaty, we have been actually aggressively supporting that kind of thing ourselves.

"For example, year before last in the movement against the security treaty our position was that we wanted a positive relationship with the United States. But alliance with the United States would in turn aggravate our neighbor country and we thought this type of alliance would drive us into a blind alley. We are calling for realism, not for the romanticism of a dream."

His point was clear—he wanted a neutral Japan.

This, I said, was a matter for the Japanese people to decide —not me. I explained that there were divergent views in the United States also about what our position on various matters should be.

I said: "We have groups in the United States who feel that our country has become too involved with others, that we should retreat within our own borders, that we have great natural resources, that we have great strength, that we could always protect ourselves. These groups say: 'Why should we make all this effort? It's not necessary for our survival. We could get along with just ourselves. Let every other country do what it wants. If the Soviet Union or Communist China wants to carry out their conquest of the world or capture another people by force, we shouldn't worry about that.'

"There are other people in the United States who hold the view that the answer to the whole problem is to get involved in some kind of war. Both groups are active, both groups have followings in our colleges. They are very vocal. And we feel this is part of the democratic system.

"So, when you have the viewpoint that you have, you are exercising your rights under democracy.

"I would say that the first group, which advocates that we retreat within ourselves, is a far more powerful and vocal group within the United States than the rather small fringe group that suggests or recommends the other course.

"But my point is that every kind of political position is represented. And we have to be quite frank; we have many people in the United States who do not feel that we should be involved with Japan, as the Japanese say here that they should not be involved with the United States.

"The way we feel is that the matter should be resolved in free discussions such as we are holding today. When you have a democratic system in which every view can be expressed, there is also a great responsibility imposed on the individual. This is a tremendous freedom that has been granted to us. But we have to have the responsibility to exercise it properly.

"The answer is not violence against those who disagree. The answer is to have the courage of your convictions and be willing to stand up and be counted. It doesn't do any good to retreat within yourselves and just exchange views with those who already agree with you and yell slogans and march with signs. Something more is required of people who live in a democratic system."

I felt that this was a point that many of the students of Japan had not yet come to understand. A democratic system gives freedom, but it also imposes obligations and responsibilities. In the United States, in England, in other countries with long democratic traditions, disagreements, the expression of different points of view are taken for granted. Democracy has existed for only a relatively short time in Japan. Democracy to many of the young people who lack this background and tradition is a license to do exactly as one pleases. Further, many of them feel this right exists for them but not for those who disagree with them. The results are the pickets, the slogans, the riots and the violence. These take the place of the verbal exchange, the discussions, the debate that we have here in this country. And, of course, it is the Communists who take the greatest advantage of this freedom, and who so greatly abuse their rights. This was clearly demonstrated at this meeting. They would picket, yell slogans, disrupt and, if possible, cause violence, but they refused to appear to exchange views. Unfortunately, they have led many of their colleagues, non-Communist though they might be, to believe that this is what democracy is, that this is their right under this system. If they march with a sign or turn over an automobile or throw rocks, they are exercising their rights. Only when their responsibilities are understood will we have a firm foundation for the democratic system in Japan, and against this eventuality the Communists are massing all their weapons.

A second boy went into the question of Berlin. He was disturbed because the world was divided in two. Berlin, he said, was a key point in the East-West struggle. He said that he feared that if Russia and East Germany signed a peace treaty it would interfere with the freedom of the West Germans and then what would the United States do? What could we do? he asked.

I told him that regardless of what else occurred our rights of access to Berlin would be maintained. "Certainly, the Soviets can sign a peace treaty with East Germany," I said. "That's their business. But we received certain guarantees and rights after the Second World War. These included rights of access to Berlin. They will not be abandoned. We don't lose those because of an act of the Soviet Union and East Germany. Of course, if the West Berliners decide they don't want to have anything more to do with us, that is something else again—although they took a plebiscite there some time ago and it showed some 97 or 98 percent in favor of the West staying in Berlin. I might say that we'd welcome a vote in East Berlin or East Germany, which the Soviet Union has never permitted.

"I wish your colleagues had been here. I would have liked to ask them why. Would you ask them for me?"

The next young man raised questions about why our government, while defending the cause of freedom, had friendly relationships with such countries as South Korea or Taiwan or Spain. "These governments," he said, "do not qualify as democratic. These governments are established by either autocratic power or landowners. And that is why when a democratic country supports these countries—and the United States supports these countries—that is why if South Korea is going to be called a free nation, then certainly the Soviet Union and Communist China should be called free nations."

This boy also had questions on his mind about how we could expect the U.N. to preserve peace and at the same time exclude a major world power such as Communist China. A third part of his inquiry concerned our role in the Cuban

78

incident. Here were three tough areas about which this student was deeply concerned. I was impressed. Have our own students thought enough about these matters?

On the first question of why we support certain governments, I replied that if he was suggesting that the United States determine what kind of governments should exist in each nation, that was not possible under our system.

"We don't ask every country to have exactly the same government that we have in the United States," I said. "For cultural reasons, because of their economic situation, because of some different historical development, a country may have a form of government entirely different from us. No country has exactly the same form of government as another does.

"We feel that every country may do what it likes. Some we admire more than others. The important distinction is that they are independent of foreign domination. We don't ask that every country in the world follow our foreign policy. They do exactly as they wish.

"For instance, the closest friend of the United States historically has been Great Britain. England voted for the admission of Red China, while we were against it. Can you ever imagine that happening in the Communist bloc?

"We help to give assistance to some eighty countries throughout the world. Some of them are far more democratic than others, it is true. We don't establish ourselves as the judge of what government is proper and what is not. We have even given aid to Poland because we feel that they at least have some freedom and liberties.

"So what we want in the world is nations determining their own destinies."

As for South Korea, I explained, as I had before, that it had gone through a period of bitter turmoil and that major government corruption had been revealed. The new government leaders had pledged to re-establish the country economically and thus restore political rights. I said I had confidence in this pledge and that many of the steps they were taking were required under the circumstances.

On Red China I said she had indicated that she did not choose to live in peace and so, with the majority of the countries of the world, we were opposed to her admission to the United Nations.

"Now, as far as Cuba is concerned," I continued, "Mr. Castro was supported, initially, by a vast majority of the American people. He promised to institute a democratic system and allow elections. Since then you have had these thousands of refugees that have flowed out of Cuba. They and objective reporters within Cuba say that it has become a complete police state. If you disagree with the government, you are imprisoned or shot. There is no freedom of speech, there is no freedom of the press. Any thought of having free elections has been abandoned.

"Can you possibly, as young people, support that kind of system? Is that the kind of operation that we believe in?" There was no answer.

The next spokesman for the group was an attractive young girl. She got into an area which has become a warm issue in Japan—women in politics. "In general," she said, "the Japanese women have a very low level of interest in politics. Inside a school, like my school, women are prohibited from entering into active political participation. There are schools of that type and ours is one of them. In comparison to this situation with the Japanese women, what is the political consciousness of the American women? What do they do? Could you tell us a bit about that?"

I thought immediately of the active parts my wife, my sisters, and even my mother had played in the election campaign of my brother. I answered:

"Well, I would say, first, women take a very active role in politics. It takes various forms, however.

"I would think, looking back to my brother's campaign, where he had a great number of volunteer workers across the country, that 90 percent of the talking was done by men and 90 percent of the work was done by women. So their participation made a major difference. They took an active interest and role, particularly many of the younger women."

Our time with these young people had ended. I said a word of farewell. I knew they felt concerned and disturbed about world affairs. I spoke on that point for a brief moment.

"Having not been out of college terribly long myself," I said, "I can remember that all students felt we were the ones who were active and interested and knowledgeable about politics. We felt that nobody else had the same kind of interest. Looking back, I don't think that is always true.

"I tell you, I have been very impressed in my trip throughout this country with the provocative, articulate way in which people from all walks of life have expressed themselves.

"As I say, there is only one group that I haven't been able to find. They have been very vocal also, but always at a distance.

"So, can I just express my thanks to you and say how much I have enjoyed this. I am very impressed with the way you have shown a willingness to speak up on matters that must affect us—not just as Japanese or Americans, but as people living in a very difficult world.

"I thank you, and the best to all of you."

The meeting was extremely interesting and I left greatly encouraged. I say this not because these young people identified themselves as good friends of the United States. They did not. They were not antagonistic but neither were they particularly friendly. They possessed alert, inquiring minds. They were anxious to learn. And they exhibited an intelligent and earnest concern about the future of their own country and, indeed, of mankind.

Before leaving Kyoto, Ambassador Reischauer and I visited a sake house in the middle of the city. We left our automobile and walked up a back alley and then into a small bar. There we sipped a cup of sake and talked to three professors from the university.

The conversation was most stimulating. We discussed the war, the occupation and the present state of democracy within Japan. They spoke with concern of the lack of stabilizing influences within Japanese life. There was tremendous potential for the future but a great deal depended on the example and encouragement of the United States. I talked with them as I had talked to the Prime Minister and other government officials about expanding Japanese help in the countries of Southeast Asia. A Westerner faces certain difficulties in some areas which cause fewer problems to the Japanese—disease, living conditions and, perhaps most importantly, acceptance by the local people. Obviously, this is not true everywhere, only in certain key countries. With the United States and Japan pooling their effort, money, resources and, most importantly, personnel, a great deal more could be accomplished during the 1960's than has been done in the past.

One night in Tokyo, after a meeting with businessmen, we visited with some labor leaders in another sake house. It was about 11:30 P.M. The "bartenders" were dressed in long white smocks and served the sake, which they took out of enormous barrels, in small white cups. As in Kyoto, we sat on stools, talked about the labor movement in the United States, the steel workers, the dock workers, the corruption that had been revealed in the Teamsters Union that these alert young men could not understand. They spoke of the role of a labor organization in politics and what steps could be taken to achieve more social legislation, and what they could do to overcome Communist leadership within some of their own labor unions.

At the end we were joined by some of the American newspapermen who came on the trip. The Japanese, in closing, sang their "Coal Miners' Song." We decided that we should sing for them. The only "American" song besides the National Anthem that we knew the words to was "When Irish Eyes Are Smiling." We produced a very off-key version, but it was vigorously cheered.

The Japanese labor leaders were a bright, tough-minded group of men. They reminded me a great deal of some of the officials in the Steelworkers Union whom I had met in Bethlehem, Pennsylvania.

We left Japan with a certain sadness. We had eaten snails and seaweed for breakfast and whale meat for lunch. We had slept on floors, lived through an earthquake, been thrown to the ground by judo experts and had gone ice-skating before breakfast. We had had meetings at 6:30 in the morning and at 11:30 at night, with a full schedule in between. We had visited farms and factories and sake houses. We had met government officials and factory workers. We had learned a great deal and enjoyed ourselves tremendously in the process.

First, the people had been so terribly kind to us—everyone, everywhere we went: Ambassador and Mrs. Reischauer and those associated with them in the American Embassy; the individuals who established and comprised the "R.K. Committee," who could not have been more generous of their time and their effort; the government officials; and finally, so importantly, the Japanese people, both those we met and those who waved and smiled as we moved by.

There are many problems ahead for Japan and the Japanese people. They have just begun the experiment of democracy, which requires the utmost in maturity and self-discipline. Many of the old-time stabilizing influences within Japan have disappeared. The Emperor is no longer the symbol that he was; since the war religious beliefs have been greatly weakened. Furthermore, the family unit, once such a dominant force in Japanese behavior, no longer wields its old influence.

Thus, as these energetic, bright, happy people are launched on this difficult experiment in freedom, a rudder is needed which will keep them on course as they travel through the storms ahead. Their major problem, which they recognize better than any foreigner, is whether they will have sufficient direction and stability to ride out the first squalls and hurricanes; whether the first challenge that confronts them will force the people to accept the easy solutions of a military dictator or of Communism, systems in which thinking and self-discipline are not required.

I have confidence that the Japanese people will win their struggle. A great deal depends, however, on our help and assistance, and particularly on the example that we set for them. I was amazed on my short trip at how many young Japanese political leaders did not know how to treat a question-and-answer period; how to meet people at a political rally; how to talk and exchange views with smaller groups. They learn and learn quickly, but they can use constructive assistance from us.

And in their own country, these younger political figures must be given an opportunity for responsible public expression.

A struggle between the young and the old is in full swing in Japan. Over and over again I was asked how a young political figure could get started in the United States; why young people were given so many positions of responsibility; how President Kennedy, such a young man, was able to run for office, let alone become President. On the other hand, by some of the older respected political leaders, I was told that young people were trying to move too quickly.

This conflict must be resolved. A proper solution is obviously to permit those who have ability and integrity to be given positions of responsibility no matter what their age.

We must help Japan in solving its trade problems and over-coming the prejudice that exists here in the United States and other countries of the West toward Japanese goods. They are hard-working, industrious people and should be our friends, as we should be theirs. They can be the most important influence for good in all of Asia. But they need and deserve understanding and assistance from the people of the United States.

CHAPTER 6

"*Another Field, Another Grasshopper; Another Pond, Another Fish*"

The mood in Indonesia was far different from the mood in Japan. Japan, despite its problems, is still a democracy. It has been sustained and has flourished in the post-war years under a free enterprise system.

Japan has an open competitive economy. It has a free press and complete freedom of expression. The right of dissent is clearly established. There is academic freedom of boisterous proportions and freedom of thought and ideas. This is an ancient, complicated and sophisticated society. At the same time it is a society that accepts and even promotes change and new ideas. Indonesia for many reasons is completely dissimilar in every respect. Some of the more superficial differences were apparent the moment we stepped off the plane.*

* I should point out that comparisons between Japan and Indonesia are subject to certain qualifications because the characteristics of the two countries are so different. Japan, for instance, has had centuries of existence as a national entity and generations as an industrial power; her people are homogeneous and speak the same language. Indonesia, on the other hand, is a new nation going through all the internal problems and turmoil that that entails without the several years of instruction and guidance from which Japan benefited. Further, it is made up of more than twenty racial and ethnic groups speaking a variety of dialects and tongues. (Its new language, Bahasa Indonesia, based largely on Malayan but containing words from Sanskrit, Arabic, Dutch and English, is expanding rapidly, however.) Indonesia's population is approximately the same as Japan's but it is spread over an area almost five times as large. Thus, the problems facing each nation are very different in nature.

In all the time that I spent in Japan I did not see one Japanese soldier or sailor. But from the moment we arrived in Indonesia we were aware that it is a nation under arms. Everywhere there were soldiers.

Even officials of the Justice Department were in khaki uniforms. The Attorney General, Dr. Gunawan, was in his uniform as he greeted us at the airplane.

In Japan our sponsoring group had made certain that, aside from the first day, when I made formal calls on Japanese leaders, we were completely free to meet men and women and young people of every conceivable background, every shade of political thought. The atmosphere in Indonesia was rather more restrictive.

While we were in Japan we received word that our Indonesian visit had been elevated and that we were no longer to be the guests of the Indonesian Attorney General but were to be the guests of President Sukarno. This meant, for one thing, that we would stay at the presidential palace rather than the state guests' house. It also lessened the possibility of an anti-American demonstration during our stay. The United States Embassy at Djakarta had been stoned only a few days before and many in the United States urged that our visit be canceled. But a demonstration against a guest of the President would be a demonstration against the President himself and would not be tolerated. It also meant, however, more formality.

Khrushchev had spent almost two weeks in Indonesia under the same auspices. While he traveled a great deal to the various islands, I knew that the impression he had left in some instances had not made friends for his country. He was frequently visibly bored with the Indonesian dances, the visits to the old temples. His remark to President Sukarno during a visit to a batik factory in Jogjakarta, where skilled artisans have hand-printed designs on fabric for centuries, was: "They could do it faster with machines."

But whatever impression Khrushchev left or whatever opinion the Indonesians had of America, all shades of thought were tinged by the Dutch occupation of West New Guinea.

More than a concern for poverty or hunger or disease is the irrational desire of every Indonesian—even the illiterate citizens of the farthest village of Indonesia's three-thousand-mile stretch of islands—to be rid of the Dutch in West New Guinea, or West Irian as they call it.

President Sukarno had made a number of speeches about West Irian just before our arrival in Indonesia and some of his emotional oratory clearly included threats of war. Some experts felt this was a real danger—that Sukarno might declare war even as he was inviting us to reside in his palace. Others regarded his speechmaking as pure histrionics, designed to keep the Indonesian's mind on patriotism and off his empty, growling stomach. Still others said that Sukarno was heavily committed to achieving a genuine national objective and that he wanted to accomplish this by peaceful means. However, the possibility of the use of force was not ruled out.

No one can visit Indonesia without being aware of the poverty and hunger of its men and women and children. Plainly, despite tremendous natural resources this nation is underdeveloped and very poor.

President Sukarno's greatest contribution to his country has been in the area of education. Under the rule of the Dutch very few of the Indonesians received advanced schooling. But Sukarno, himself intelligent and a fiery orator, a man with a good mind and a good education, has made at least a beginning in making his people literate. Through his efforts for Indonesian independence, Sukarno is the symbol of free Indonesia to the Indonesian people.

I was most anxious to be able to have frank discussions with as many students and student groups as possible. Clearly, these young people, like those in Japan, are going to make the difference in the years ahead. They will shoulder the burden of the further development of their nation. Their country's future and the choice between freedom or reversion to colonialism—this time a type imposed by the Communists—are in their hands. If Western democracy is to be understood in Indonesia, it will be because its students of today come to have some understanding of our way of life, our ideals and our goals.

Our stay at Istana Negara, Sukarno's palace, was an interesting one. We did not see the President on the day of our arrival, but we paid a courtesy call the following afternoon. He generously invited us and the members of our party—including members of the American press—to attend a private dance exhibition to be given by his fourteen-year-old daughter, Megawati, the next evening. His daughter, a lovely and talented girl, performed one of the native Indonesian dances which are so famous the world over and which we greatly enjoyed.

My first chance to speak to the youth of Indonesia came on the morning after our arrival in Djakarta. I was to deliver a lecture to the student senate and the faculty of law at the University of Indonesia. Approximately a thousand students were to attend.

The nearest thing to an incident in Indonesia occurred as I entered the hall at the university. The place was completely surrounded, as was always the case everywhere we went in this country, by troops and police. As I stepped onto a porch at the entrance, a tall, skinny young man, clad in summer white, stepped suddenly through the lines of soldiers. He took a full windup and let fly at my face with a piece of hard-shelled fruit. It hit me on the bridge of the nose, but aside from the sudden jolt of it, I was unhurt and continued into the school building to deliver the address. Police seized the youth and hustled him away.

In one way it was a cowardly act since I was, for the moment, defenseless. And yet, thinking back on it, I was struck by his complete political dedication and the difficulties we in a democracy have in matching it. Here was a young man who knew that his efforts to injure me would result in his immediate arrest. Still, his desire to do anything he could to take a blow at an "American imperialist" overshadowed everything else.

Had there been any doubt in my mind that the question of the dispute with the Dutch was the burning issue on the minds of the Indonesians, it was immediately dispelled by the student who introduced me. He recited my biography, concluding with a reference to the book I had written in 1960. Then he launched into a most unusual introduction, telling me my visit coincided with the "important West Irian question," and that in this case the Indonesian students did not want to be, and would not be, left out. "Mr. Attorney General," he wound up, "in your program the Netherlands is scheduled to be the next country you will visit. You will please send our regards to the students of the Netherlands and tell them that we, the students of Indonesia, are standing by waiting only for President Sukarno's final command. It is true that we love peace but we love our freedom more. Thank you."

It was clear that the applause which echoed in the room as I took the rostrum was meant for the young man.

I thought, for a moment, of attempting to deal directly with this subject but decided that it would be a mistake. So I stuck to my text.

I felt it was a better answer, in the long run, to tell these young people that their history and the history of the United States had striking similarities; that as they were revolutionaries, we Americans were the heirs of the true revolution from colonialism. I wanted them to know what our country has stood for in the past—and stands for today.

I also wanted to put Indonesia's problems and aspirations into perspective in relation to the rest of the world and the forces that were shaping it today. This is what I said, in part, on this subject:

". . . The outstanding spirit abroad in the world today is nationalism—nationalism closely linked with anti-colonialism. Nationalism itself, of course, is nothing new.

"This self-determination performed the essential function of giving people an identity with their country and with each other. It became in some societies, not merely an article of faith and common aspiration, but also a badge of conquest.

"This was true of the nationalism which characterized the old Roman Empire, and was the driving force behind the German, Italian and Japanese dictatorships in the days before World War II. It has not been true of our American nationalism.

"Nor is it true of the new nationalism loose in the world today. This nationalism has taken the form of 'nonconquest,' of disengagement from former economic and political ties.

"It is re-creating in many parts of the world a sense of identity and of national aims and aspirations that the old order had too often sought to stifle.

"The United States has always been sympathetic with this kind of national aspiration. . . .

"We have sought to aid new nations with technical

and financial assistance during their crucial early years. Our aim is that they survive, develop, and remain proud and independent. . . .

"The United States has no desire to impose its conception of the role other nations should be allowed to assume. And I can tell you quite frankly we have no intention of permitting any other nation to enforce its system on other nations of the world.

"On the contrary, the answer we have given and shall continue to give calls, as President Kennedy said, for the association of nations on a world and on a regional basis to defend the rights of the least in behalf of the whole.

"The rise of the new nationalism has been coincidental with the struggle against colonialism. Anticolonialism is one side of the coin whose opposite side is nationalism. . . .

"But anticolonialism is nothing if it does not follow national paths and remain true to its basic principles. If anticolonialism is the struggle for freedom, then the new nations must remain free. . . .

"Your President, in striving for an increase of living standards, has set as his goal 'a just and prosperous society.'

"Its attainment, even to a moderate degree, is difficult. Men may differ as to what form of government will do the best job. Even within independent governments such as yours and mine, there is no rigid formula upon which all of us can agree. . . .

"You have a saying in your country: 'Lain ladang, lain belalang; lain lubuk, lain ikan'—'Another field, another grasshopper; another pond, another fish.' Or, in other words, each country has its own customs and habits. . . .

"As in any society, there are improvements that can be made, problems that remain unsolved. We Americans have not fully attained for ourselves the prosperity that we seek for our people and all mankind.

"We can do better and we intend to do so. Our struggles against racial discrimination, our continuing struggle against want, our efforts to lift the levels of education so that any man may choose freely in the light of knowledge, all these struggles will continue.

"But we are making progress with them. That is what is important. We will not accept the *status quo*.

"Another force released by World War II can be designated as the revolt against economic feudalism. It has other names as well, such as economic betterment or the necessity for industrialization or agrarian reform. This, too, is part of your goal of a 'just and prosperous society.'

"All the forces set in motion as a result of World War II are, and continue to be, forces for freedom throughout the world—freedom from foreign domination, whatever its form; freedom from the economic cares of want: freedom to achieve, to solve one's own problems, to think and do and act for oneself; freedom from fear, from violence and from the hopelessness which has so often accompanied poverty.

"We in the United States regard highly the importance of private incentive. We see it as a mainspring for social action. This does not mean that state enterprise is incompatible with freedom. Our public power, our nuclear energy development and similar undertakings are proof that we can utilize, where desirable, the credit of the state in lieu of private capital.

"But our history has been primarily that of private enterprise—controlled by the government wherever necessary in the public interest.

"No other nation to my knowledge has left the development and ownership of its transportation systems, both rails and airlines, or its communication system in private hands.

"We have had time and the resources to do so. Other nations may not have time to wait or the resources to do so. But the degree of private and public control is not the test of freedom, either economic or political.

"Complete economic activity by the state can stifle freedom, but the point at which a balance is struck between the use of promoting the two methods of producing wealth will vary from time to time and from nation to nation.

"I say this because we have no desire to fasten our economic image upon any civilization. We think the balance between these two areas of activity must be based

91

on experience. It must be hammered out in the light of the culture and resources of a particular nation and is not to be answered by a doctrinaire ideology which, far from being revolutionary, is a new feudalism that enslaves rather than frees.

"The important factor, and the one to which we are committed, is that the state exists for man, that man is not a tool of the state.

"It is difficult for me to understand why the opposite ideology could appeal to any peace-loving nation or to a nation that takes—and rightly takes—a fierce pride in its independence.

"At home this ideology subjugates the individual to the state.

"On the international scene it looks to the envelopment of nations into a system which it must control. Divergence of views, either at home or abroad, cannot be tolerated. Of these perils, we have sought to make our friends aware. Against them we offer no set ideology, no patent means of government, but an emphasis on individual dignity and a program of opportunity and assistance in terms of friendship.

"I cannot leave this platform without remarking on the great problems that face us in the world today and the role that young people must play in achieving their solution. The younger men and women will have to live longer with these problems and will have to find new answers year after year, in every field—in government, in politics, in business, in the sciences, in the arts.

"The great challenges of these years, the responsibilities that now must be met, provide greater incentive and greater opportunity than ever before for the educated young people of our world.

"Education is more than merely giving an individual an economic advance over his neighbor, over those who are less fortunate.

"We have obligations and responsibilities to our fellow citizens, to our country, indeed to the people of the entire world in these days when we are all each other's neighbors. We have responsibilities to encourage and spread the dedication to independence and to freedom.

in the Coast Guard. There are now Negroes in the Coast Guard Academy.

"He went out to review the Honor Guard, walking with a newly elected President of one of the African states, and observed there wasn't one Negro in the Honor Guard. That has been changed.

"For the first time in the history of the United States, three District Court judges who are Negroes have been appointed for life. The two top law enforcement officials in Cleveland and San Francisco, appointed by the Federal Government, are Negroes.

"All of the bus terminals in the United States that handle interstate transportation have been desegregated, and that amounts to well over a hundred bus terminals. More than two hundred railroad terminals have been desegregated in the United States."

I told them that "a major effort has been made to hire Negroes in all departments of the government; again, not just because they are Negroes, but because they are qualified to perform jobs, that the President has announced that if his plan for a Department of Urban Affairs is passed by Congress, he intends to appoint a man to head it by the name of Weaver, who happens to be a Negro. It would be the first time a Negro has served in the Cabinet of a President of the United States.

"A number of sub-Cabinet positions are already held by Negroes.

"We are going to have problems," I told them. "There will be a great number of other incidents, as at the time of the freedom riders. There will be people beaten up. But these incidents wouldn't occur if we weren't trying to move ahead, refusing to accept the *status quo*.

"But the important thing is that the President of the United States wants to make progress. The Administration desires to make progress, and the vast majority of the American people are backing that effort.

"So we will make progress. But I ask from you some tolerance of our problem. There are customs and mores that have been built up for several hundreds of years in certain parts of the United States and they cannot be broken down overnight, cannot be changed just by snapping a finger.

There has to be a change in men's hearts." There were then a number of other long questions on West New Guinea. I attempted to answer them with patience and repeatedly explained the position of the United States and its interest in having purposeful discussions to resolve the issue. On and on we went.

One questioner had a bite as well as some sarcasm in his voice. He wanted to know what the U.S. would do to preserve peace if negotiations between the Indonesians and Dutch broke down. He knew that it was Indonesia which had so far refused to go to the conference table without certain preconditions and had threatened force if their demands were not met. Therefore, if negotiations were not successful, the acts of aggression would undoubtedly originate with Indonesia, and this young student wanted to goad me into making an anti-Indonesian statement or a remark that would compromise the United States. "I am hopeful," I replied, "that negotiations will not break down, but if they did, our attitude would be very much determined by who was responsible for the breakdown." By this time I was becoming slightly impatient. Many of the questioners had given me long lectures before they asked their questions and, for the most part, they were clearly, or by implication, critical of the United States or of its policy of not siding with Indonesia in this dispute. I decided to take note of this now, so I added:

"There is a good deal of criticism in Indonesia about the United States' position on this matter. We have allies throughout the world, and we don't agree with everything that they do, and they don't agree with everything that we do. I don't know of any of you who agree with every one of your fellow students. You have disagreements. You have disagreements among the various people that live here in Indonesia. But you don't suddenly say that they are disloyal, or that that shows that they are not for democracy, because you disagree with them.

"We disagree with England. We disagree with France. I suppose a day doesn't go by when we don't disagree with the English on some matter or other. We are going to disagree with Indonesia, and you are going to disagree with us.

"But we are both democratic countries. We both should have a foundation of friendship, so that every time an incident comes up and we don't do exactly what you want us to do, you don't say, 'To hell with the United States.'

"I mean there has to be a little more maturity. I will tell you quite frankly that the vast majority of the American people didn't like what happened at the Belgrade Conference of 'neutral' nations. But this doesn't mean that we are suddenly all going to pick up our marbles and go home.

"We are different people. We are separated by ten thousand miles. There was a good deal of feeling in the United States that as Attorney General I shouldn't come to Indonesia because of the incidents that have occurred here. But the President and the Administration and the vast majority of the American people felt that we should come and that we should try to make a greater effort to understand one another. And that is part of the role that I am playing here.

"But I also ask for some understanding on your part. This is not a one-way street, ladies and gentlemen."

Strangely enough, it was this answer more than any other that seemed to establish a friendly rapport with the audience. There was a vigorous ovation, and it at last ended any further discussion of West New Guinea at that session.

We turned to a different subject—and this put me into more trouble than anything on the trip.

The question came from a smiling young man who had dug into his history books and written out his question so as not to forget it.

"Your Excellency," he began, "the subject I am going to bring up won't deal with the remarks you made just now in your speech, but rather with a piece of history of your great country. I hope you won't mind, sir."

"I haven't minded so far," I said, "thank you."

"That piece of history of your country which I have in mind concerns the Presidential election of 1844," he went on.

"Oh, I do mind," I said, amidst laughter.

But he persisted.

"Well, I know you are an expert on elections, sir. In 1844, the Democratic party, the party that now controls the White House as well as Capitol Hill, extended into the arena of the Presidential election with this slogan, and I quote, 'Fifty-four forty or fight.' The Democratic party won the election and Mr. James Knox Polk became President.

"As for the 'fifty-four forty' fight, it didn't materialize.

"Now, sir, the questions I am going to ask you are these: First, whether the Americans were justified in their claim vis-á-vis the British. And as I indicated before, the 'fifty-four forty' fight never materialized; but let's suppose that the British won the fight. Are such fights now considered just and honorable? Would you care to comment on that?"

"That is a very unfair question," I answered, amidst more laughter and applause for the question. "First, I don't think, looking back on it, that there would be a great deal of support for the position of the Democratic platform at that time that we were justified in claiming up to 'fifty-four forty.' * And I think it was realized by Thomas Benton and others, who were very vocal initially, that we really didn't have a very good position, and that it should be resolved in other ways.

"So then we went into discussions, and through peaceful negotiations we were able to resolve the matter, and to everybody's satisfaction. So we didn't have a war with the British at that time, and peaceful discussions won out, and I think it was most fortunate."

I think they got the point. At least, they applauded vigorously.

The next question was the one that caused the difficulty. It came from the same boy.

"Although the 'fifty-four forty' fight didn't materialize, the Mexican War did. So I think that—well, when peaceful negotiations might break down, as one of my fellow students has brought forward—well, what should be the alternative, sir?"

I replied—in what turned out to be a massive understatement—that although there might be someone from Texas who might disagree, I would say that we were unjustified in the war with Mexico. "I don't think that this is a very bright page in American history, the war with Mexico, and I don't think we were justified in getting involved in it; and I think there are some questions about certain other matters we have done in our history. But I don't think that that is one of which we can be particularly proud."

That about closed the meeting. I presented to the univer-

* Some important historians believe that the "fifty-four forty" slogan was not in fact used until 1845, but the "spirit" of the slogan was present during the 1844 election.

sity the first collection of some five hundred books that the United States was donating through our aid program. The students were extremely warm, enthusiastic and friendly. I did much better with them than I did with some of the Texans. I did not realize how much of a storm had been created until a week or so later when I read some back editions of U.S. papers, and saw I was being bitterly excoriated by some of my Texan friends. Also, Pierre Salinger sent a cable from Washington saying:

YOUR REMARKS ABOUT TEXAS APPEAR TO BE CAUSING SOME FUSS. IF YOU ARE PRESSED ON THIS MATTER, PRESIDENT SUGGESTS YOU ATTEMPT TO MAKE SOME HUMOROUS REMARK. GOOD LUCK.

When I arrived back in the United States I said after meeting with the President that, although I was not being "muzzled," I had been instructed in the future to clear all my Texas speeches with the Vice-President.

Also, after I arrived back I was flooded with books, letters and pamphlets—whatever the senders thought was appropriate—about the history of Texas. All of them gave very sound accounts of the Alamo and the fight of Texans for their independence from Mexico, but many of them contained very little or nothing about the U.S.-Mexican War. I thought that in itself was interesting. In fact, a number of those castigating me publicly, including many Congressmen and other political leaders, did not even have the correct war.

I had only one meeting with union officials in Indonesia. It was in Djakarta and was not eventful. There is little industry in this country and labor has small impact on society. A group of about twenty-five of them came to see me at the office of the Labor Minister. They were placid—almost subdued. I had the feeling that someone perhaps had suggested that they refrain from asking any questions so as not to embarrass a guest. Whether or not this was the case, they asked few questions. We found very little to talk about. Once again, as in Japan, none of the Communist labor leaders appeared, although they were invited.

CHAPTER 7

"Capitalism" Is the Dirty Word of the Orient

President Sukarno urges all visitors to his country to travel across Indonesia and see some of the different islands, and he provided three airplanes for our trip. We were to go to Jogjakarta, to Bali and then to Bandung. On the last day of our stay we were to drive to the mountain retreat of the President, Bogor, and have breakfast with Sukarno and his wife.

At each place scheduled for a stop I tried to arrange a session with students and other young people. At Gadjah Mada University in Jogjakarta, on the first leg of our flight, I spoke to approximately a thousand students. The Attorney General of Indonesia was a graduate of Gadjah Mada and accompanied me to the hall where I was to speak.

I had been told originally that a brief off-the-cuff address would be appreciated and that there was no need for a prepared text. However, when we arrived at Jogjakarta the night before, we learned a text was expected—and a lengthy one. And so that night I put together an address with the help of excerpts from some of my speeches in Japan as well as the one in Djakarta.

Communications media in Indonesia are not developed. There is no mass communication. Newspaper circulation is insignificant. There is no television. Radio broadcasting still is not advanced technically. Even the telephone system is troublesome to operate. For this reason I felt that many of the same points I had made two days before at the University of Indonesia would bear repeating here at Jogjakarta.

In sessions I had held with various groups I had discovered

100

a misunderstanding of our own federal system and the division between federal and state rights, so I decided to touch on it in my talk here. After speaking of our common interests, our revolutionary heritage and the progress being made at home as we strive to live in real freedom, I went on to tell something of our form of constitutional government.

"In the United States we have a federal system and this creates some problems and difficulties in our efforts to make progress. There are areas of action where the states are dominant and the Federal Government is powerless. There are other areas which the states cannot invade. The political destinies of states are never all controlled by the same political party, and their political outlook can differ state by state from that of the national Administration. This makes for problems and difficulties in realizing certain national goals. In civil rights matters, our Federal Government has a direct responsibility to combat discrimination in voting but can move against discrimination in transportation only when the interstate transportation system is involved. The Federal Government can intervene directly in school desegregation cases only at the direction of the federal courts.

"Thus constitutional barriers can impede efforts at the national level. However, our achievements in steadily decreasing discrimination have been significant. Furthermore, the conscience of America has been deeply stirred. In the states and in society as a whole progress is plainly apparent. We in the nation's capital will encourage this with all the resources that we possess."

In closing I spoke of the need to combine restraint and responsibility with freedom.

The comprehension of English was not so good as it had been in Djakarta, although I was told that no interpreter was needed. In the question period following, after finding some of my answers were not fully understood, I suggested an interpreter be used. As usual, the principal issue was West New Guinea. My first interrogator came to the microphone with his questions written out in advance. He began to read them and had completed ten of them in rapid-fire order (he had sixteen in all) before there was a chance to interrupt and to say that I couldn't possibly remember everything he had asked.

On West New Guinea, the questions and my answers were

much the same as they had been at the University of Indonesia.

Did I acknowledge that West Irian belongs to the Republic of Indonesia? Did I believe that Indonesia could expect to get West Irian this year? Why had the United States not supported the Indonesians in the last session of the U.N.? Our position, he said, gave him the impression that the United States of America was reluctant or afraid to support Indonesia on the West Irian question. Did I agree with him that our position favoring neither side would make bad relations between the United States of America and the Republic of Indonesia?

Many questions he asked were repetitious. At one point he asked a second time what we would do if the Dutch sent troops to West Irian. I said: "Didn't I just answer that question?"

He replied: "Yes. I would like to ask the question twenty times."

He finally worked down to his last question: "Could you suggest, please, how should we struggle to get West Irian as soon as possible?"

"Sit down and have negotiations with the Dutch."

Even this exchange did not satisfy these students. There were additional inquiries about the same subject. Finally one of the young men went to a different subject: "Is it true that the United States of America is a capitalistic monopolistic country and that monopolistic capitalism competes with our form of socialism?"

As he spoke the words "monopolistic capitalism" there was a burst of applause. When the question was completed, the student returned to his seat.

It was clear from this question that here, as in Japan, there was a total misunderstanding of our society. Speaking directly to the particular young man, I said: "You said that we are monopolistic and capitalistic. These phrases were used in your question in an uncomplimentary fashion. Tell me what you mean."

He remained in his seat.

I then asked him to come forward and tell me and the rest of the audience what he had in mind. He refused. I asked for any of the students who had laughed or applauded at the use of the expression to come up and tell me and the audience in what way that description fitted the United States. Not one of them volunteered. I told them they had a representative of the United States in their midst and now was the time to discuss this matter, to state their disagreements or even dislikes, and not after I had left. Not one of them would accept the challenge. So I went on to say again that I'd welcome any specific criticism with which I could deal directly.

Once again I pointed out that ours was not the same country as that of a hundred years ago when we were going through a period of industrialization and transition. I repeated what I had said at Djakarta—that we had made mistakes but that we were not standing on the past or accepting the *status quo*, that we were moving ahead in many areas, that we provided for our people as no other society was able to do. Then I said, "I want to make sure that you don't just become slaves to slogans. I know that a good number of students here have many questions about the United States. And I would be wrong to say we are without fault. But we are working toward solving our problems. We are moving in many areas. An individual in the United States has the right to join a union and organize it and strike against his employer.

"Our press is free.

"Our political parties can organize.

"We have taken tremendous steps in the field of education. We still have far to go. But this is not the society that was described by Marx or is criticized by the Communists here in Indonesia."

And then I went on to point out, as I had in the past, that, unlike the Communists, we were not attempting to impose our system of government on any other country; we wanted to see a diversity of nations, all determining their own destiny and acknowledging a common responsibility to all mankind.

The interpreter visibly cringed at my criticism of the Communists. At first it appeared that he would not translate it, and it was only at my prodding and specific request that he finally did.

This student, with his question and statement, which were supported by the vast majority of the audience, was Mr. Iwai, the labor leader of Japan, all over again. Here were the same misconceptions and misunderstandings and the same acceptance of the Communist slogans. "Capitalism" is the dirty word of the Orient and we are the victims of our failure to correct the record with a realistic presentation of how our economic and social system works. And added to the misunderstandings are the problems in the United States for which we have still not found the complete solutions and which are almost incomprehensible in many areas of the globe.

Racial discrimination is the problem which evokes the most attention and interest. In Jogjakarta, as everywhere else, I was asked about racial difficulties within the United States. I answered as I had before. I said we had made progress, we would continue to make progress, but we would have difficulties and, perhaps, acts of violence in the future before we found a full solution. The audience on this subject, here as elsewhere, listened but could not fully understand.

The audience at Jogjakarta, as at Djakarta, warmed up considerably by the end of the question period. The exchange was vigorous and interesting, and to me, at least, most helpful. To once again feel and hear what was bothering the future leaders of this country regarding the policies of the United States and its people was an invaluable experience. Unless we understand these people, which also involves understanding their attitude toward us, we cannot possibly develop programs which can maintain our position of leadership throughout the world.

While in Jogjakarta we were the guests of Sultan Hamengku Bowono IX, a man now past his middle years, who is one of the most respected leaders of the islands. It seemed strange to be meeting a sultan in his palace at this time in history. However, he retains a unique position in Indonesia. The son of a wealthy old family, he was a large landowner at the time of the revolution for independence— and he was one of the few people of property who vigorously participated in the war for freedom from Dutch colonialism. Once Sukarno's Defense Minister, he now heads Indonesia's Tourist Bureau. He lives in the large palace which was formerly occupied by the Dutch and it was there that we stayed as his guests.

He now walks with a cane, but he kept pace with the vigorous schedule arranged for us in Jogjakarta. We all visited the cultural landmarks in his area, which included a magnificent temple seven centuries old.

In both Jogjakarta and Bali we were entertained by famous Indonesian dancers. Perhaps the most arresting was a symbolic dance of the Balinese in which male dancers go into a deep trance and stick themselves with razor-sharp swords. The hypnosis is so effective that frequently the performers don't bleed. Our energetic and able Ambassador, Howard P. Jones, told me the doctors have no medical explanation for this phenomenon. It was a dramatic and impressive but also rather horrifying spectacle.

On the evening of our arrival in Bali we were the guests of the government at a hotel cottage on a beautiful beach. I went for a long walk and on my way back to the cottage a young man walked up to me and challenged me to a running race. I was surprised but I accepted. And so we raced. It was another fine gesture of Indonesian hospitality—he allowed me to win.

We went for a late afternoon swim in the surf. With the heat and humidity as great as it was, these moments of relaxation were doubly appreciated. I could not help but think, and later observed to several officials of the government, that the free enterprise system here could be a major help to the people. The investment of capital in modern hotels along the beach—hotels that would attract thousands of tourists each year—could boost the economy substantially.

The answer I received was the same answer whenever we suggested that a free economy, or at least a free economy in the tradition of many socialist countries, could bring major benefits to the people. "We are just not ready for that yet," they told us. "In the future perhaps such things can be done."

I don't know how long the future will wait. The Dutch left the people unprepared, with inadequate training and insufficient education, and it is no wonder that substantial progress has not been made. In fact, many of the Dutch thought the country would collapse after their departure. It has not, and the young people are being trained, but in the meantime many things could be accomplished for the welfare and benefit of the people which are not being done.

The leadership here, as in many former colonial areas, has

a natural mistrust of the free economic system. This is the system that exploited them and they believe that this is what will happen again. They don't realize that in certain sectors of their economy a free enterprise system with built-in controls to protect the Indonesian people, and established for their benefit and not for foreigners and outsiders, could be most helpful. It is only when this is understood that substantial gains will be made. This kind of effort supplementing governmental activities is essential for the full development of a country with as many possibilities and potentialities as Indonesia enjoys. However, the full impact of the implications of the words "capitalism" or "free enterprise system" came back to haunt me when I spoke at the University of Bandung the following day.

Naturally, I was anxious to go to Bandung, the scene of the first of the famous conferences of the neutral nations, and visit the building where an important piece of world history had been enacted.

We left Bali on Friday afternoon; the weather was cloudy and the three-hour flight was turbulent. Our party now included many ranking officials of Indonesia as well as members of the press. We were still traveling on the three planes furnished by President Sukarno. Two of these were American-made Convairs, the other was a Russian model of our Convair made in Czechoslovakia. Ethel and I and the other members of the official party were assigned to the Communist-made aircraft, while the members of the press and the rest flew in the American Convairs.

The two American planes made the flight without difficulty, but our pilot, after circling and flying for about six hours, decided that because of inadequate equipment we could not get through to Bandung. He made more than six passes at Bandung before finally going on to Djakarta. We heard later that he felt that his inability to get us in would be considered a tremendous loss of face in view of the success of the other two planes. In fact, I was told afterward in a rather joking fashion that at the very moment he was telling us that he had given up the attempt to land at Bandung and that we were on our way to Djakarta, actually he was making another attempt through the mountains to land us at Bandung. I managed a smile.

Early the next morning I boarded one of the American

planes and a short time later landed in Bandung. Even though I could have only a few hours in the city, I was anxious to make the trip because a visit had been arranged to the Bandung Institute of Technology. This was the university from which Sukarno himself had graduated at a time when it was operated by the Dutch and so it was of particular interest.

Upon arrival I visited the Conference Hall, toured the market place and received some presents from the local military commanders and the Governor, including a large stuffed lizard for my son Bobby. Somehow they had found out how much he likes animals.

The university had planned an outdoor meeting. The students were seated in a wide circle, approximately seventy-five yards from where the rostrum was placed. I urged the school officials to permit them to come closer so that we might have a more informal meeting. There were about a thousand of them, and they picked up their chairs and rushed forward, delighted with the change in arrangements.

Almost immediately I ran into that haunting word that causes us major problems all over Asia—"capitalism." The student leader who introduced me was very friendly. But early in his remarks he mentioned that the Indonesian revolution had been against "imperialism and colonialism." Several times he repeated those words—"imperialism and colonialism." Then—almost, it appeared, without realizing it—he began to use the word "capitalism" interchangeably with both "imperialism" and "colonialism." At one point he said: "In our struggle against imperialism and capitalism . . ."

And again he commented that he hoped that the United States "in the spirit of Thomas Jefferson" would "show a firm position against colonialism and capitalism."

When he had finished and I had been introduced, I asked him what he understood the word "capitalism" to mean. He seemed completely dumfounded and literally had no answer.

In much of Asia the word "capitalism," because it was the system used to exploit the people, is an evil word, and the Communists have spared no effort in reminding people of this fact. They also remind them that the United States has the capitalistic system and, therefore, if given the opportunity, would renew this system of exploitation. We, on the other hand, have just not faced up to the fact that we have to convince people that what they understand as capitalism is not in any way the kind, form or system of government existing in the United States or indeed in most of the Western nations today. We have to get back to the fundamentals of our beliefs, our ideals, and demonstrate how we apply them in our approach to our everyday problems. We must establish that our system of government is not only not one of exploitation, but, to the contrary, has as its ideal freedom and unselfishness.

I had no prepared text for my appearance at the university. I spoke from a few notes I had made that morning on the airplane. My speech was relatively short and after a few minutes I opened the meeting to questions.

This group, as it turned out, was the most open-minded, the most uninhibited and the most plain-spoken of any I met with in Indonesia. I greatly enjoyed it.

I told them that I was not there to spread propaganda but that I had expected to arrive the night before. I had been over Bandung the previous evening in a Russian plane, which had to turn back because of weather. Two American planes which had been in our party and left at the same time arrived safely. They laughed and applauded when I said that though the Russians might get to the moon they could not get us to Bandung.

In a more serious vein I said that the young man who had introduced me had remarked, "We don't want to be the last generation on this earth." I said our aspirations are identical. "Our generation in the United States doesn't want to be the last generation on earth either."

The questions were probing, even though, as might be expected, I had been asked many of them before. The first questioner said that both the United States and the Communists were interested in world peace, and wasn't there then an identical objective and purpose in our two systems? Weren't we very much alike? he asked.

I said plainly that I could not agree. "The Communists," I replied, "are interested in peace only when it serves their purpose. Their objectives are far different from ours. They will take any steps, internal subversion or external force, in order to achieve control of a country. It is only the strength of a number of countries around the world that has kept the peace.

"I think, for instance, that if the United States were to disarm, you would have problems far greater than those that exist now in the world. . . . The Soviet system and the system of democracy are far, far different.

"There are other fundamental differences," I added. "In our country everybody thinks of a better way of running the United States than the President and that he or she would be an improvement over the President—at least on some matters.

"But that is what we welcome, different ideas and different viewpoints. But they cannot have that under the Communist system. That is a basic difference.

"Think of what happened to Mr. Pasternak when he wrote a book which took a different approach and was critical of his government. He was not allowed to receive the Nobel award. How could that happen under a democratic system?

"Can we really compare that system with our system, the democratic system, where you can have differences of viewpoint? In fact, let me say this. If you don't like what is happening in your country or in my country, you can get out. This certainly is a difference.

"I cannot admit to that premise that we are both interested in the same thing.

"I think as long as the Soviet Union or the Communists recognize that if there is atomic war it means immense destruction all around the globe, they will want peace, of a sort.

"But to say that peace is their philosophy—I would differ quite strongly with that."

They, too, asked why the United States opposes having Red China in the United Nations.

I reminded them that we had had a major struggle in 1951, 1952 and 1953 in Korea in which some fifty thousand men were killed and because of that there is a good deal of bitterness in the United States against Red China.

"Despite that," I reminded them, "the President has indicated that if the attitude of Red China should alter—if they should show by their actions that they are willing to live in peace with the United States and with the other countries of the Free World—our attitude and, I am sure, the attitude of other countries would also change."

I called to their attention the fact that the Chinese are still holding American prisoners—and that, further, they have announced their policy to be the destruction of the United States.

"We are concerned and disturbed about their activities. We are far from convinced that they want to live in peace. They have not indicated any willingness to abide by the precepts of the United Nations."

Another student noted that I had been traveling across his country for some days. "We will ask you frankly what impression you have now," he said.

"I think there is a tremendous potential here," I replied. "You have greater natural resources than many countries of the world. They should be used and developed for the benefit of the people. If you dedicate yourself to that, you are fulfilling your responsibility.

"Things that impress me most are the efforts that have been made to educate the young people. I think you were left unprepared. I was told as I came up to Bandung that there were only two hundred university students in the whole of Bandung before the war and only a hundred of those were Indonesian. Now that a major effort has been made some twenty thousand young people have been educated in this area.

"That means this country is going to play a greater and greater role throughout the world. Indonesia has an important position at the present time, as you know. But it came on the world scene with many of the young people unprepared and without education. Now you have a system which can take care of that.

"You, like the young people of my country, must realize that the purpose of an education is not just to gain an economic advantage over your neighbor who has been less fortunate. Education means far more than that. You must make a contribution to your people, to your community and to your government. That is your responsibility."

This group was one of the most enthusiastic that I have ever seen anywhere. They were happy, they laughed, and we all thoroughly enjoyed ourselves. They followed me down to where my car was parked, surrounded it, waved their hands and yelled pro-American expressions. They also gave me a present of an album before I left. I thanked them and said, amidst laughter, I was sorry I was not in a position to give them West New Guinea in return. Hundreds of them followed my car out into the street.

I left Bandung immediately after this meeting to fly back to Djakarta. My stay in this country was coming to a close, but there were meetings with government leaders and others scheduled up until the time of our departure.

During one of the brief afternoon lulls in our schedule, I left the palace at Djakarta to walk through the streets and shake hands with the people in the shopping area nearby. I entered an Indonesian bookstore and walked among the shelves observing the books on display. It was not a happy experience. There were a number of English textbooks of a highly technical nature—but no books on American history, none on the American Government; none of our novelists or poets were represented, and there was not one book by the President of the United States. There were books about Russia, about their leaders and about their astronauts. Here clearly we were missing an opportunity to make our system known to these people. The operator of the bookstore said he would be glad to display our books, but so few were offered to him.

The remarks I had heard in Japan—that the Communists were beating us to the punch in cultural exchange—came home with impact here in Indonesia.

In Djakarta, Attorney General Gunawan gave a large dinner for all of us at which we were entertained by Indonesians doing the unique Candle Dance. Afterward I suggested that we should show an example of an authentic American dance. The Attorney General agreed and I called upon Susan Wilson, who was assigned to the trip by the *Ladies' Home Journal* to write an article about Ethel, and Brandon Grove, representing the State Department, to demonstrate the Twist. Susie obliged brilliantly, while Brandon, mumbling bitterly about his Image in the Department, produced a genteel and polished Charleston.

It was a great success, and many of the rather staid and serious Indonesians joined in, while the Attorney General confided in me that the Twist had been banned in Djakarta.

After the dinner, John Seigenthaler went to the American Embassy to see about mimeographed copies of my speeches, and when he returned to the palace at about two in the morning he found he had no identification, and the guards refused to let him in. He finally persuaded one of them to let him go as far as the room he was sharing with Brandon Grove, assuring him that Brandon would identify him. While the guard stared stonily he shook Brandon, who finally sat straight up in his bed and said, "I've never seen that man before in my life." John got very little sleep that night. Brandon had thought the dance exhibition idea was his.

I had a final meeting with President Sukarno at his mountain palace at Bogor, an hour's drive from Djakarta. He was affable and friendly as he welcomed us to this scenic retreat. He did say, fortunately with a smile, that he was aware that several dozen times during our visit I had said the United States was a close friend of Holland's.

Deer roamed across his front lawn. Giant bats nested in a huge tree near the gate to his property. He escorted us through the palace and showed us the only painting he has ever done, that of the face of a woman. I thought it was very good—better than some by other more famous painters which were hanging in the palace.

We had a meeting for several hours on the West New Guinea question. This was the second long conference on the matter, and in addition to President Sukarno, Ambassador Jones and John Seigenthaler, Foreign Minister Subandrio, who is extremely able, and Sukarno's First Minister Djuanda, in whom he reposes the greatest confidence, attended. We met around a large table in President Sukarno's office and made a good deal of progress.

Sukarno was not anxious to spill the blood of his people nor to undertake the expense of an armed conflict unnecessarily, although he was determined that the administration of West New Guinea be eventually placed in the hands of the Indonesians.

Before I left we came to an agreement that he would send negotiators to meet with the Dutch to determine if the matter could be solved amicably. This was at least a step forward, although I could see many hurdles in the future. We were not dealing with completely reasonable men on either side of this controversy.*

We drove back to Djakarta and began to pack our bags to leave. A half hour before our departure, I met with a group of young leaders and students who came to see me at the palace. There were approximately thirty in the group and their ages ranged from the late teens to the mid-thirties. Their faces reflected intelligence and interest, but for the most part they were shy and showed no inclination to speak out. Only five or six among them had anything to say. Three of them were very aggressive and I suspected that they represented Communist organizations (this was verified afterward).

The most outspoken of the group, who later identified himself as a leader of the Communist youth group, was very critical of what he called the United States' support of colonialism. Why did we not take a stand with Indonesia against the colonialism of the Dutch? he asked insistently. This young man—in his mid-thirties and a member of the Indonesian Parliament—did not want to accept the fact that the Dutch were anxious to leave West New Guinea and might be willing to negotiate with the Indonesians as to its future. He clearly indicated he felt war with the Netherlands was the only answer.

I said to him, "You know it is always easier to say, 'Well, let's go to war,' over things. War now can have very wide ramifications and the President of the United States has said again and again that he is going to go the last mile to try to avoid any conflict as far as our country and as far as any other part of the world is concerned."

One of his colleagues said colonialism is amoral, and that this fact should be realized and accepted by us. He said we should join with them and oppose colonialism wherever we might find it.

* Some time later the representatives of Indonesia and the Netherlands did meet for several days just outside Washington. Progress was made, but eventually, because, in my judgment, of the intransigent and stubborn position of individuals on both sides, the discussions were not continued. I shall always have hope that the uselessness of a conflict will be recognized and negotiations will be reopened.

I was interested in learning if the few who were speaking out were against colonialism—or if they were propagandizing. I said to them: "Accepting that premise—accepting the fact that colonialism is amoral and should be opposed everywhere in the world—do you oppose the Chinese in Tibet, the Russians in Latvia, Lithuania and Estonia, or the Russians' activities in Hungary? Let me hear from you on that. Let's find out if you are truly against colonialism."

Their leading spokesman said, "We want to talk about West Irian—not these matters."

"I know you want to talk about West Irian," I replied. "I have given you my position on West Irian. Now I want to find out about your positions on some other matters. Are you in favor of what the Chinese did in Tibet?"

"Let us talk of West Irian."

"I thought that somebody said he was against colonialism and I just wanted to find out how far that went. Are you just against colonialism in West Irian or are you against colonialism in Hungary; are you against the Russians' sending their troops in there? Are you against colonialism in Poland and Eastern Europe?"

The answer came. "We believe in these instances the governments involved have the full support of the people."

"Well, then, how do you explain the wall in Berlin? This is a wall that was erected not to keep invaders out but to keep their own people in. If these governments have the support of the people, why do they have to erect a wall? How do you explain that?"

"We don't want to discuss details. We want to talk about West Irian," was the answer.

I received no support from any member of this group. And on this note the meeting broke up. I went to my room and finished my packing. Twenty minutes later when I came out, four or five of the young people were waiting for me. We chatted amicably for a few minutes. They were obviously not part of the Communist group and asked friendly, inquisitive questions about the United States. I learned later that they had remarked to several of the American reporters that I was absolutely correct about Communist colonialism. Anthony Lewis of the *New York Times* asked them why they hadn't spoken up. They answered quite directly that this was just not done in youth groups. No one criticized Communism. No one defended the West.

The students had been intimidated, and, as I subsequently learned, this happens in many of the "new" nations; which leaves the field wide open to the Communists. This is a fact that we must face, that we must understand, but it is a situation which we need not and cannot accept. To do so, to accept the *status quo*, to admit we cannot reverse the situation, is to admit defeat, to accept disaster. There is much that we can do. The important thing is that we begin.

Indonesia has immense potential—in its natural resources, but most of all in its people. They need to be given an opportunity to express themselves and to get their country moving forward. The chance of success in the future will be far greater if the West New Guinea issue is resolved peacefully without pouring still more of Indonesia's wealth into its war machine. To a considerable extent the future of that part of the world depends on how this dispute is handled.

I have said that in every country I visited I discovered deep sources of goodwill toward the United States. There were anti-American reactions of sorts—in Japan and Indonesia—but these represented a minority point of view. By and large there was friendship—not understanding, perhaps, but real affection for the American Government and people.

A poll was taken in Japan shortly before my visit. It showed that the most popular foreign country was the United States, the most unpopular the Soviet Union. In Indonesia President Sukarno took the various ambassadors with him on a trip through the islands around the first of the year. He introduced each of the ambassadors to the crowds. Ambassador Jones invariably received the biggest welcome and loudest cheers, while the Russian and Chinese representatives were far down the list.

This is certainly not conclusive evidence of American popularity, and, at least as far as Indonesia is concerned, this popularity is partially due to the personal impression that Ambassador Jones has made on the Indonesian people, who hold him in the highest esteem.

However, everywhere we went on this trip, people gathered to greet us. In Japan the tremendous press coverage given to foreign guests brings out huge numbers of spectators. And they were friendly Japanese crowds, laughing and happy people living in a free society and glad and proud of their accomplishments.

They could not have been more complimentary to Ethel and me. They swarmed over sidewalks and roadsides everywhere we went, even in the rural areas. In the later days of our visit I could hear them shout out to me as we passed: "Hi, Bobby, where's Ethel?"

There were crowds, too, in Indonesia. They were also friendly and, frequently, enthusiastically so, but generally, by comparison, lacked the zest and enthusiasm of the Japanese people. Sometimes I even had the impression that they had been told by the authorities to stand by the roadside and wave as we passed. Certainly, none were unfriendly, but the real warmth which we experienced in Japan was missing. They never really seemed involved in our trip. However, from time to time we would break away from the troop guards which sought to keep us from harm as well as on schedule, and would simply walk through the crowds to shake hands and greet them. Always this brought smiles and friendly words in return.

Indonesia contains some of the oldest identifiable races of people on earth, as well as a culture that has been developing for many hundreds, if not thousands, of years. When we visited one of the temples in Bali, the guide told us they had been able to erect it in "less than a hundred years." It struck me then, and later on the plane, how short a time in history a few decades or even a lifetime is. Communism has been in existence in the Soviet Union for only half the time that it took to erect this temple in Bali (and a far shorter time in China), and yet both Russia and China are now facing tremendous internal upheavals and problems.

How difficult it will be to subjugate over any extended period of time a people such as these Indonesians, with their thirst for knowledge and the eagerness of the young people to make progress.

Just before we left the palace Attorney General Gunawan came to our room and gave Ethel and me a huge, ferocious-looking tiger (stuffed). John Seigenthaler refused to carry it on the plane and so we shipped it home by sea.

There was a large crowd at the airport. We were all reluctant to say good-bye to many who even in a short time had become friends.

CHAPTER 8

"Something There Is That Doesn't Love a Wall . . ."

—Frost, "Mending Wall"

Heart-warming as our reception in Japan had been, the crowds in West Berlin were unlike any that I have ever seen. I have traveled a good deal in the United States and around the world. I campaigned in 1960 all across the nation and so I have seen crowds in all parts of this country as well as abroad.

Never have I been so moved by crowds as I was in Berlin. The welcome we received in that city affected by so much suffering and so much anguish is something we can never forget. It was not merely that by turning out in large numbers they demonstrated affection and trust, nor was their waving merely a gesture of greeting. It was all this, but it was more. Through their numbers, through their waving, through their tears, they wanted to tell the American people, through us, that they depended on the United States—not on the French, not on the English, but on the United States—and that without the United States they felt they were dead and West Berlin was dead. This was the message.

It was below freezing when we arrived, and snow was falling. We were met by General Clay, Mayor Brandt and others. I reviewed the Honor Guard (as Ethel whispered, "For a Seaman Second Class, you've come a long way"), gave a short arrival speech in German which I had memorized phonetically, and then we drove into the city. A hundred thousand people lined the streets as we drove from the airport.

Mayor Brandt and I rode in an open car. I saw old men and women standing side by side, waving their handker-

chiefs and their hats, tears streaming down their faces, plain-
tively crying out: "Hello, American, hello."

Here were people, who twenty years ago waged all-out
war against us, now standing in the snow, baring their hearts
and their heads to let us know they were depending on us
for their freedom and for their very existence.

On the way in from the airport we stopped briefly to look
at the wall which lies like a snake for twenty-six miles across
the heart of Berlin, separating families and friends not only
from personal contact but indeed from communication in
any form. It is impossible simply by reading about it to
understand the revulsion it stirs. It cuts off streets, it tears
across open fields, it consumes apartments and churches and
makes even them part of the barrier.

Along the way there are places where monuments have
been erected on the sidewalks in memory of those who died
fleeing the Communists. These monuments are vivid reminders that there are those still who prefer death on free soil to
life under tyranny.

As we neared the City Hall of Berlin en route from the
airport, the number of people lining the sidewalks increased.
And when we arrived in City Hall square, there were an
estimated 180,000 people packed in the court, overflowing
across the streets and jamming the sidewalks.

This was where I was to speak. I had worked for several
weeks before leaving the United States on a speech to be
given at the Free University of Berlin that evening. It was
not until boarding the plane in Rome that I learned of this
address at the public square. The State Department had prepared a brief formal statement for my appearance there. I
found that it did not suit me and so I worked on some ideas
and gave the speech from notes.

I had trouble beginning my speech—I was so cold I had
difficulty saying the first words. I had just come from an extremely warm climate and had not adjusted to the freezing
weather. Further, I had lost my overcoat in Hong Kong, and
though they had sent me another one in Rome from the
United States, it turned out to be my father's, purchased
before the war. It was not a very warm one, and on top of
all this, I had just been driving in an open car. So, as I stood
up in front of that vast multitude of people, I was shaking
so hard that speaking was extremely difficult. Ethel saved

118

the day by coming up behind me and unobtrusively rubbing my back, which gave me enough warmth to get through the short speech.

"Over the past few weeks my wife and I have traveled many thousands of miles across the United States, across the Pacific Ocean, from Japan along the Chinese coast, down to Indonesia, across the Indian Ocean, across Pakistan, up through the Middle East, through Italy, and now we arrive in the free city of Berlin. Nothing we have seen has touched us as much as your reception for us here today.

"The warmth of your greetings will always remain indelibly in our hearts, and the message it gives is one that I will report back to the American people. And I want to report to you that it is reciprocated by friendship and affection for the people of Berlin and admiration for your great courage.

"So I am proud to be here in the city of Berlin. This is my third visit to your city. I came here first in 1948 during the Berlin airlift. It was when Berliners and Americans were standing side by side. General Clay and your Mayor, Ernst Reuter, stood shoulder to shoulder when the Communists attempted to bring the proud city of Berlin to its knees. On that trip I traveled not only to West Berlin but to Communist East Berlin, and the contrast between Communism and freedom was there for all to see. And I saw it for myself.

"But on my return in 1955, I came from a long trip through the Soviet Union and I came here to West Berlin and saw your pleasant streets and gay shops and your fine people. And when I went over to East Berlin, again it was like returning to a bad dream."

Suddenly my talk was interrupted by loud explosions as the Communists set off two rockets. They soared directly over the square and burst in the sky above us. Four red flags floated down on balloons. The crowd booed and hissed in anger.

I pointed up to the floating balloons and said: "The Communists will let the balloons through but they won't let their people come through."

119

The roar of support from the crowd must have echoed in Mr. Ulbricht's house across the wall. I continued:

"I have seen the contrast between this city in the West part and in the Communist part, as many hundreds of thousands of people have seen that contrast. And that is why Herr Ulbricht had to erect the wall. Because it was a contrast that he could not tolerate.

"That is the true meaning of the wall that lies like a snake across the heart of your city. Mr. Ulbricht and the Communists cannot afford the contrast.

"He cannot tolerate the contrast between freedom here and Communism over there so that everyone can see it. He has had to erect the wall. We are aware of the heartbreak and anguish this wall has caused to the people of Berlin. But I would also ask you to look at the other side and see what an impression it has made all across the rest of the globe. Because this wall is an admission of failure by Communism. It is an attempt for the first time in the history of mankind to erect a wall, not to keep marauders or bandits out, but to keep their people in.

"And this incident has been repeated over and over again in my travels.

"If the purpose of the wall was to destroy Berlin, Herr Ulbricht and his cohorts have erred sadly. Berlin is not only going to continue to exist—it's going to grow and grow and grow.

"Its ties to West Germany will not be severed. Companies from America and other foreign countries will erect their plants here. Corporations from all over the globe are going to open outlets in this city. West Berlin's brightest pages have yet to be written in the books of history. And Berlin, although on the edge of totalitarianism, will not be attacked, because an armed attack on West Berlin is the same as an armed attack on Chicago, or New York, or London, or Paris.

"You are our brothers and we stand by you.

"And now I have a message from President Kennedy to you of free Berlin. It is to Mayor Brandt, the Senate and the people of West Berlin.

" 'I am delighted to send my warmest greetings to the

people of West Berlin through my brother, the Attorney General of the United States. His visit to Berlin is one more testimonial to the ties that bind your city and the American people. I am grateful to you for having invited him, and the message which he brings is the message of American solidarity with the free people of West Berlin. The courage and determination of the people of your great city are a constant inspiration to free men everywhere. Our people and yours have stood firm for freedom in the years that lie behind us; together with other determined peoples we shall sustain both freedom and peace in the years ahead.' "

When I finished these remarks we went inside the City Hall with the Mayor, upstairs to the second floor and out onto an open balcony looking down over the square. The mass of people were still standing there in the bitter cold, looking up, and they again greeted us with a moving ovation that echoed and re-echoed across the square to the walls on the other side. Both Ethel and I were deeply touched.

Then with Mayor Brandt we went inside, where officials of his city were gathered. We were grateful for the brandy, hot coffee, sweaters and boots offered us. Ethel and I performed the traditional ceremony of signing the Golden Book of the City.

Willy Brandt is a courageous leader. He has a firm will, a tenacious spirit, an alert mind and—a necessary asset for any politician—a strong voice. When he speaks, one has the feeling he truly represents the strength that has molded the character of this city.

The image of Willy Brandt has become the image of Free Berlin all around the globe.

After the Golden Book ceremony, the Mayor presented us with a small china statue of a bear—the symbol of his city. I thanked him for this gift as well as the replica of the Freedom Bell* and expressed our gratitude once again for the welcome we had received.

The morning after our arrival, we left Ambassador Dowl-

* A replica of our Liberty Bell, which was given to the people of Berlin by the People of America on United Nations Day, October 24, 1950, by General Lucius D. Clay. The Berliners call it the "Freedom Bell."

ing's house in Dahlem to meet Mayor Brandt at the Brandenburg Gate. The weather had warmed slightly but it was still a gray, cold day with the temperature in the high twenties. Even so, crowds of people gathered on street corners and along our route, waving white handkerchiefs and shouting greetings. Several times the crowd was so thick that the cars were slowed to a crawl as women thrust bouquets of flowers into our hands.

Mayor Brandt and his attractive wife Ruth, who is Norwegian and fought against the Nazis with him in the underground, were waiting for us at the Brandenburg Gate. The famous gate, a symbol of German power in the past, is just inside the East Zone. Ulbricht's gray wall curves in front of it. The West Berliners have erected a wooden tower so that visitors can see over the wall. My wife and I climbed to the observation platform and we could look out into East Berlin, which was deserted except for a few East German police and three photographers who took pictures of us with long-range-lens cameras from their side of the wall.

I could not imagine what they were going to do with the pictures. Nor could anyone else that I asked. They were, however, very conscientious in their work. There was a time when the Russians would permit East German photographers to come near the gate and even into the Western sector. But since three of them defected, they now must take their pictures a hundred yards from the other side of the wall.

An hour before we arrived at the wall, a Soviet honor guard entered West Berlin for a ceremony at the Russian war memorial, which is a sort distance from the Brandenburg Gate in the British sector. We did not meet, but Mayor Brandt pointed out that the British thought it necessary to erect barbed wire around the Russian memorial to protect it from possible damage.

During this second look at the wall, I said to Mayor Brandt, "In addition to the anguish this causes you, you must have such contempt for those in the Eastern Zone who are responsible. Looking across at the East German guard, don't you feel that those people have betrayed their countrymen in a way that perhaps can never be forgiven?" In answering he spoke of his determination and the determination of his fellow Berliners that the wall shall come down, and that all

Berlin shall one day be free. He talked of the problems the Russians have had in obtaining guards because so many of them had fled to the West. Now they try to select men who come from deep inside East Germany and who have families still living there. Further, in many of the more critical spots, they place a guard to watch the regular guard and then place another guard to watch him. "It is," he said, "but a small minority of the population who voluntarily support Ulbricht and the Communists."

I had an opportunity to talk to one of the several hundred guards who had successfully fled East Berlin. He was a young boy in his early twenties. He said most of his fellow police would flee but it was far more dangerous and difficult now, and frequently for any kind of safety at least one of the other policemen must be brought in on the plan. He said they now move the police around so often that you not only have no chance to become sufficiently familiar with a particular place where a break could be made, but you have no one you can trust.

Upon leaving the Brandenburg Gate, Ethel and I parted. She and Mrs. Brandt visited a German-American community school and West Berlin's largest department store. Mayor Brandt and I headed for Bernauerstrasse, a street running parallel to the boundary between the French and Soviet zones. The street and sidewalks remain in West Berlin. The buildings on the southeast side of the street are in East Berlin.

In the early weeks after the wall was built, many Berliners escaped through these buildings. They jumped from windows four and five stories high to nets held by West Berlin firemen. A few persons missed the nets and died, and the sites of these tragedies have been marked by crosses. The East German authorities barricaded the buildings and walled up the doors and ground-floor windows, and later bricked up the windows on all the floors. Now and again someone still risks his life and tunnels to freedom or leaps from a building top into a net or crashes through the wall with a car or truck amidst an East German fusilade of Russian bullets.

Bernauerstrasse was a drab and relatively unknown street before August 13, when the wall sent up. Now it is a symbol of the determination of the West Berliners to be free and of the East Berliners to seek freedom.

I placed a wreath at the cross marking the place where Frau Ida Siekmann jumped to her death in September of 1961. Photographers and reporters crowded around and as the brief ceremony was completed the newsmen left and momentarily I was standing alone. I turned and could see the upper stories of several apartments across the wall in East Berlin at the end of the street. Women watched from the windows and Communist guards peered over the wall. As I turned, several of the women slowly and carefully waved their hands without moving their arms. It was a poignant moment and I felt a chill in the back of my neck.

From the street where persons seeking freedom had jumped to their deaths to escape Communism, we drove to Ploetzensee, a part of a prison where anti-Nazi resistance leaders were executed for their part in the unsuccessful plot of July 20, 1944, to assassinate Hitler and overthrow the Nazi Government. The car stopped outside the prison wall. As we entered, we walked between two large groups of school children forming a semicircle around the outside wall of the building which serves as part of the memorial. The air was chilly and the sky gray, and the children and their teachers and the adults present remained silent, adding to the solemnity of the situation. I laid a wreath at the base of the wall and then spoke briefly about how moving it had been to drive along the wall and see the ashamed look on the faces of the Communist guards, to see people at windows in East Berlin waving surreptitiously and contrasting with the magnificent expressions of courage and hope on the faces of the people of West Berlin.

"I laid a wreath there honoring the victims of Communist tyranny," I said, "and have now come here to place a wreath in honor of those who are victims of Nazi tyranny. This, I believe, demonstrates what all of us here stand for . . . and in the final analysis what we must carry away from here, namely, that people, no matter where they live or what be their mode of life, will not consent that the state or a single group of persons should decide whether an individual may enjoy the liberties that were given to him by God. . . ."

Hitler had ordered that the six resistance leaders be "strung up like pigs." They had been taken to a butchershop near where I laid the wreath and were executed. The six hooks which were used to carry out this dreadful deed re-

124

main today in the shadowy building as grim reminders of
the depth of Nazi depravity. Mrs. Julius Leber, whose hus-
band was one of the six executed, met me. She told me that
she was grateful that Americans still remembered that there
were brave Germans who opposed Hitler and died in the
struggle against Nazism. She took my arm as we looked at
the hooks. Before I took her back to the car, I tried to tell
her how touched I had been by what I experienced that
morning.

After the visit to Bernauerstrasse, we undertook a far
lighter and more pleasant task. We visited the Berlin Zoo and
there presented an American bald eagle to the people of Berlin as a gift from the people of the United States. I
conscripted two reluctant bird-bearers, John Seigenthaler
and Ed Guthman, from the Department of Justice, who had
joined our party, to carry the eagle from the entrance of
the zoo to an open cage which had been prepared for it. By
now, Mrs. Brandt and Ethel had rejoined us, and we made
the presentation from inside the cage. We released the eagle
and he flew to the top of the cage, curled his claws around
the wire, spread his wings and glared haughtily down upon
us. We named the huge bird "Willy Brandt" because, like our
American eagle, Mayor Brandt is a symbol of strength,
courage and liberty.

Mayor Brandt's American counterpart in Berlin was
General Lucius Clay, who is a hero to the Berliners. General
Clay symbolizes the courage and determination of the Berlin
airlift. In returning to Berlin as the President's representative
in the tense days immediately after the wall was erected, he
gave that city new hope and preserved their courage. As I
said in my farewell speech at the airport, he has been an inspiration to Berliners and Americans alike.

The main purpose of my visit to Berlin was to deliver the
Ernst Reuter Lecture at the Free University of Berlin. Ernst
Reuter, Willy Brandt's predecessor, had been Mayor of that
city during its most perilous period—that of the Berlin airlift. His name stands for freedom in West Berlin. He was
loved and followed by his people and despised by the Communists, whose threats and authoritarian order he laughed
at and ignored.

The Free University was founded in December, 1948, a

few days after the Soviets had formally split the city administration. In the old Berlin University in the Soviet sector
discrimination against non-Communist students had increased to such a point that many of the faculty and a large
number of the students simply walked out of the university
and founded their own institution, which they called, with
good reason, the Free University.

At its beginning it functioned in dark, unheated, inadequate and scattered buildings, released from requisitioning
by the American forces. Thanks to the help of the Ford
Foundation and the backing of General Clay and other
Americans, it has today a sprawling campus with modern
buildings, offers doctorates in six faculties and has a student
body of over twelve thousand.

Its reputation among other European universities is high.
It has sponsored the Ernst Reuter Lectures since the death
of Mayor Reuter in 1953.

I felt it was most important in this lecture, which com-
memorates a man who was willing to compete with the
Communists in their own front yard, to point up the results
of competition in other areas of the world where the results
were just as definite though less dramatic.

For while the wall dramatically testifies to the defeat the
Communists admit to in Berlin, there are more subtle, but
nonetheless devastating, examples of victory for the West
in other areas of the world. This was what I was thinking
of as I prepared this lecture. Mayor and Mrs. Brandt gave a
dinner for our party before the talk. We had been joined in
Berlin by my brother Edward and he also attended the dinner as a guest. It was his birthday as well as George Washington's and the Brandts were thoughtful enough to present
him with a cake and several other gifts. We sang some songs
and then from the dinner we all drove across the city to the
Free University.

The lecture was given in a large hall that normally ac-
commodates eight hundred people, although that evening
more than a thousand students and guests crowded the auditorium. My wife and I walked into the hall with Mayor
Brandt, General Clay and Mrs. Reuter. The students clapped
and stamped their feet.

After a brief salutation I said:

"Ernst Reuter has become a twentieth-century symbol of liberty, and his cause enlists the active support of nations like my own, thousands of miles from the Brandenburg Gate.

"Let no one mistake the firmness of our commitment to this cause. Our position with regard to Berlin is well known but, to remove all doubt, let me reaffirm its essential elements today.

"We have stood in the past—and we will stand in the future—for the full freedom of the inhabitants of West Berlin and for the continuation of West Berlin's ties with the Federal Republic and the world beyond.

"We have stood in the past—and we will stand in the future—for the presence of Allied forces in West Berlin, as long as they are necessary and as long as you so desire. We will not allow this presence to be diluted or replaced.

"We have stood in the past—and we will stand in the future—for an active, viable West Berlin. Berlin will not merely exist. It will grow and prosper.

"We stand behind all these positions with the full strength of American power. I am glad to have the opportunity today to reaffirm the solemn statement of the President of the United States: 'We do not want to fight but we have fought before. We cannot and will not permit the Communists to drive us out of Berlin, gradually or by force.'

"We do not feel that the maintenance of the integrity of West Berlin threatens any legitimate interests of the Soviet Union, and we remain confident that, in due course, this problem will be resolved through the processes of peaceful negotiation. The flowering of this great city will be the most fitting of all memorials to Ernst Reuter.

"We have not forgotten the men and women of East Berlin and East Germany. We know the hardships they endure under a harsh and repressive regime. We look forward to the eventual reunion of Germans in freedom. For the first time in the history of mankind, a political system has had to construct a barrier to keep its people in, and the whole world recognizes the desperate meaning of this act.

127

"They wall their people in.

"We set our people free.

"Robert Frost, who read from his poetry at the Inauguration of our President, once wrote these lines:

> *Before I built a wall I'd ask to know*
> *What I was walling in or walling out,*
> *And to whom I was like to give offense.*
> *Something there is that doesn't love a wall,*
> *That wants it down.*

"What wants this wall down is the whole free spirit of man.

"The statistics on the flight of scholars offers us an idea of what Communism has done to this free spirit. Since 1958, a total of 1,606 scholars—mainly teachers in the humanities and sciences at long-established universities and technical institutes in East Germany—have left the Eastern Zone and registered in West German reception camps. More than half are members of faculties. One hundred and eighteen of them are full-fledged professors—a number equal to the professorial component of East Germany's third largest university, at Halle. In the last four years, Halle has lost a total of 147 faculty members—more than the current size of its teaching staff. Humboldt University has lost 275 members of its staff; Leipzig, 199; and so on down the list.

"As the chief law officer of the American Government, I am particularly interested to note, too, the flight of many judges and lawyers from East Germany.

"The wall is more than a demonstration of Communist failure in the struggle for men's faith and hope: It is equally a desperate effort to stem the tide of unification in democratic Europe. By attempting to isolate West Berlin, the Communists hope to subtract West Berlin from West Germany and then to separate West Germany from Western Europe; and, by subtracting West Germany from Western Europe, they hope to defeat and wreck the great cooperative instrumentalities of the regathering of democratic strength, the Common Market, OECD and NATO.

"I can assure you that the wall will fail as spectacularly in this purpose as it has failed to seal off Communist Europe from the magnetic attraction of democratic Europe.

"Ernst Reuter said a dozen years ago, 'Here in Berlin all the slogans that rend the air during the East-West struggle take on a real meaning. Here no one needs any professional lectures about democracy, about freedom and all the other nice things that there are in the world. Here one has lived all of that; one lives it every day and every hour.'

"Freedom by itself is not enough.

"'Freedom is a good horse,' said Matthew Arnold, 'but a horse is to ride somewhere.'

"Ernst Reuter knew that what mattered finally was the use to which men put freedom—that what counts is how liberty becomes the means of opportunity and growth and justice.

"We do not stand here in Berlin just because we are against Communism. We stand here because we have a positive and progressive vision of the possibilities of free society—because we see freedom as the instrumentality of social progress and social justice—because Communism itself is but the symptom and consequence of the fundamental evils, ignorance, disease, hunger and want, and freedom has shown mankind the most effective way to destroy these ancient antagonists.

"The free way of life proposes ends, but it does not prescribe means.

"It assumes that people, and nations, will often think differently—have the full right to do so—and that diversity is the source of progress. It believes that men advance by discussion, by debate, by trial and by error.

"It believes that the best ideas come, not from edict and ideology, but from free inquiry and free experiment; and it regards dissent, not as treason to the state, but as the tested mechanism of social progress.

"It knows that diverse nations will find diverse roads to the general goal of political independence and economic growth. It regards the free individual as the source of creativity, and believes that it is the role of the state to serve him, and not his role to serve the state.

"I come to Berlin from thousands of miles of travel through Asia. I have seen men and women at work building modern societies so that their people can begin to share in the blessings of science and technology and become full members of the twentieth century. Social progress and social justice, in my judgment, are not something apart from freedom; they are the fulfillment of freedom. The obligation of free men is to use their opportunities to improve the welfare of their fellow human beings. This, at least, has been the tradition of democratic freedom in America. It will be the permanent effort of Americans—and it is the specific purpose of this Administration—to keep moving ever forward until we can realize the promise of American life for all our citizens, and make what contribution we can to assist other peoples to win justice and progress and independence for themselves.

"Every free nation has the capacity to open up its own new frontiers of social welfare and social justice. Communist leaders have sometimes spoken of peaceful competition as to which society serves the people best.

"Here in this city lies an answer to the question of competition. It is an answer so overpowering that it has had to be shut from sight by concrete and barbed wire, tanks and machine guns, dogs and guards. The competition has resulted in so disastrous a defeat for Communism that the Communists felt they had no alternative but the wall.

"We find the same answer all over the world. Few countries were as devastated by the war as was Japan. She alone suffered from nuclear attack. Her great industrial cities, Tokyo and Osaka, were in ruins when she surrendered. No comparable city in China endured comparable destruction. Peking, Shanghai, Canton, Hankow —all were left substantially intact.

"Yet today Japan, which I visited two weeks ago, has a thriving economy. Her standard of living is higher than that of any nation in the Far East. Her ships roam the far seas, and her airlines fly from Tokyo to New York and London. Communist China, on the other hand, suffers in her fifth year of hunger. The tragic "commune" experiment has collapsed. Industrial production has slowed down. Poverty and disease stalk the land. Even worse, thousands of innocent people have been imprisoned and killed, and the more fortunate have fled to other lands, more than a million to Hong Kong alone.

"Communism everywhere has paid the price of rigidity and dogmatism. Freedom has the strength of compassion and flexibility. It has, above all, the strength of intellectual honesty. We do not claim to know all the answers; we make no pretense of infallibility. And we know this to be a sign, not of weakness, but of power.

"The proof of the power of freedom lies in the fact that Communism has always flinched from competition in the field where it counts most—the competition of ideas.

"The flight of scholars and jurists from East Germany shows the fate of intellectual freedom under Communism. To this day—nearly half a century after the Russian Revolution—one virtually never sees on a Moscow newsstand any magazine or newspaper exported from a democracy except Communist party publications. Yet one is free in Washington and London and Paris to buy all the copies of *Pravda* and *Izvestia* one wants.

"When will the Communists be confident enough of their ideas to expose them to the competition of democratic ideas? I was disappointed to note that only a few days ago a Russian leader, while saying that coexistence with democratic social systems was possible, asserted emphatically that coexistence with democratic ideas was 'impossible and unthinkable.'

"It would amount, he said to Communist ideological disarmament. I would have thought that he might have more faith in the capacity of Communist ideas to survive such competition; but he may well be right in fearing to let Communism stand on its own in a free forum.

"President Kennedy, since his inauguration, has steadily sought new ways and means of increasing the exchange of ideas with the Soviet Union. This is why he has been ready to arrange interviews and to offer our full courtesies and facilities in return.

"We proudly press the challenge: let the ideas of freedom have the same circulation in Communist states that Communist ideas have in free states. We can have formal peace without such reciprocal competition in the realm of ideas; but until we have full freedom of intellectual exchange, I see no prospect of a genuine and final relaxation of world tension.

"Marx's condemnation of the heartless laissez-faire capitalism of the early nineteenth century now—by an irony of history—applies with fantastic precision to twentieth-century Communism.

"It is Communism, not free society, which is dominated by what the Yugoslav Communist Milovan Djilas has called the New Class—the class of party bosses and bureaucrats, who acquire not only privileges but an exemption from criticism which would be unimaginable in democratic society. Far from being a classless society, Communism is governed by an elite as steadfast in its determination to maintain its prerogatives as any oligarchy known to history.

"And it is Communism, not free society, which has become the favorite twentieth-century means of disciplining the masses, repressing consumption and denying the workers the full produce of their labor.

"By this historical paradox, it is free society, and not Communism, which seems most likely to realize Marx's old hope of the emancipation of man and the achievement of an age of universal abundance.

"If freedom makes social progress possible, so social progress strengthens and enlarges freedom. The two are inseparable partners in the great adventure of humanity; they are the sources of the world-wide revolutionary movement of our epoch. This movement, of which Ernst Reuter is a contemporary hero, did not begin in the twentieth century. It began two thousand years ago in Judea, and I like to believe that it took its modern form in 1776 in the American colonies.

"In some parts of the world today the Communists seek to capture that revolution. But it is always stronger than those who would subvert and betray it. It is stronger in arms—and the determination, if necessary, to use them. And it is stronger because it expresses the deepest instincts of man.

"President Kennedy said recently, 'Above all else, let us remember, however serious the outlook, however harsh the task, the one great irreversible trend in the

132

history of the world is on the side of liberty.' He added, 'And we for all time to come are on that side.' His speech was addressed to Americans, but I know that he would wish me to apply it here, as he does, in his own mind, to all the world.

"You know that you do not stand alone. President Kennedy made our position unmistakably clear to the world when he said your freedom 'would not be surrendered to force or through appeasement.'

"And that is the position of our allies as well. As an official and a representative of the United States Government, I am proud of that stand and I salute the men who lead you and have so bravely carried on in behalf of our common ideals. And, as an admirer of your courage and your determination, we salute you, the people of Berlin, and we wish you well."

It is impossible to drive through the city of Berlin and put the torture of World War II out of your mind. For the scars of war are everywhere. Bullet holes still pockmark buildings along the thoroughfares. Structures which were going up during the time of the bombings still stand unfinished. Here and there monuments, ripped apart by bomb fragments, still stand as stark reminders of the flaming hell this city was when Hitler's tyranny crumbled. Yet I could not help but notice the amazing transformation that had occurred here in the fourteen years since I first visited Berlin —new structures for former gutted buildings, the people prosperous-looking and brightly dressed. The pain and suffering that haunted their faces in 1948 have largely disappeared, although occasionally one sees a look of apprehension or concern.

Courage today is a commonplace characteristic in Berlin. I saw it on the faces of the people in crowds; I saw it in the soldierly actions of the American troops when I visited the Third Battle Group; and I heard about it firsthand from two young students who had voluntarily undergone incredible risks to bring people out of East Berlin. These young men came to see me at seven in the morning. I had arranged for the visit with some Americans who had been long-time supporters of the Free University. These students and their friends had organized what was, in effect, an underground railway, using the sewers and other means to go back into East Berlin and guide people to freedom. They said they had received messages from people in all parts of East Germany seeking some way out. They were handsome, young, strong-looking, and committed to continue their efforts until they were imprisoned or shot. Because they are not alone and because of their courage, their determination, their unselfishness, we shall win in this struggle. They are the answer to that Japanese union member who asked me about the corruption of an affluent society.

Another thing that struck me was the attitude of the Berliners toward the United States. It was perhaps best illustrated by an incident in a large market hall in the working-class district of Moabit. I had been scheduled to go there in the morning, but the visit was canceled without my knowledge when we began to run behind schedule. When I was told that more than ten thousand people had been waiting, I sent word to Mayor Brandt that if he could meet me there I would return to the market in the afternoon.

We arrived at 5:00 P.M. A huge crowd stood outside. Mayor Brandt was waiting at the door. We tried to go inside to visit some of the vendors but it was almost impossible. The crowd was tightly jammed shoulder to shoulder. With the help of the police, we were able to get about fifty feet into the market. Then it was obvious that someone was going to be crushed.

Since the door through which we entered was jammed with people, we pushed our way to a freight elevator, descended into the basement and exited out a side door. The crowd on the street had by this time increased, and they now numbered in the tens of thousands, completely stopping up all the streets leading to the market place. We made our way to a police truck which had a loudspeaker system. Mayor Brandt and I spoke and the crowd responded by singing West Germany's anthem. It was an incredible experience, standing atop that truck listening to those thousands of voices.

We later had an opportunity to meet with some of the labor leaders of West Berlin. We visited together in a rather elaborate German tavern. We drank beer and exchanged views and facts about the labor movements in our two countries. They were very anxious that President Kennedy should come to Berlin and address their members and I promised to convey their invitation to him. Only a relatively small percentage of the workers of Berlin are enrolled in unions, for the laws and regulations of organizing make this work far more difficult than in the United States. However, they are determined to continue their efforts. They are staunch friends of the United States and dedicated anti-Communists.

Before leaving Berlin, we visited Checkpoint Charlie, which is the only border crossing left in the American Sector. With Mayor and Mrs. Brandt we walked to the line which separates the two zones. Five or six unsmiling Communist guards, unarmed, stood a few feet away. They were all officers, for the Communists were going to take no chances of anyone's escaping from the East during our visit. Again, as far as we could see into East Berlin, from the windows and the rooftops, people leaned out and waved to us.

I left Berlin with the memory of strong faces—on the streets in West Berlin and framed in the windows across the wall.

CHAPTER 9

The Young at Heart

We flew in military helicopters to Bonn. I scarcely looked out the windows as we flew the 110 miles over East Germany, for I needed the time to prepare for my next meetings and discussions.

In Berlin we had stayed at Ambassador Dowling's residence, which he virtually turned over to us. He and his wife were in Bonn and were kind enough to ask us to stay with them at the Embassy there.

The contrast between Bonn and Berlin—in the atmosphere, people's faces, in the general outlook of the citizens—is apparent immediately. In Bonn the strain, the pressure, just does not exist. A visit to this city is like stopping at a small river community in the United States. The people have confidence in themselves, in Germany, in the future. Well dressed and prosperous-looking, they are not particularly affected by the problems of the world outside. The emotion, the zeal, the enthusiasm, the involvement of Berlin are lacking. It was like entering an entirely different world.

The two main purposes in going to Bonn were to see Chancellor Adenauer and to address the West German Society of Foreign Affairs.

I had met Chancellor Adenauer briefly in Washington on one of his earlier visits and had been struck, as must be everyone, by his alert mind and strong, tough, almost Asian features. We had exchanged only a few words at the first meeting and so I looked forward with great anticipation to seeing him for a longer period of time. It was to his office that I went immediately upon arrival in Bonn.

Our plane from Berlin arrived on schedule. After a ten-minute helicopter ride across the city to a small field, and an arrival statement before a few hundred people and the press, Ambassador Dowling and I then drove off to the Chancellor's office. He met us just inside the door, asked us into a room for pictures, and then took me up to his office on the second floor to have our talk, which lasted almost two hours. His interpreter was the only other person present.

The newspapers during this time had been full of reports and "leaks" that the Germans, and particularly Adenauer, were distressed about United States policy and activities in foreign affairs. These stories claimed that highly placed German officials were reporting that Adenauer and others felt the United States was backing down on Berlin and was making important concessions to the Russians on Germany. The State Department, therefore, felt that this visit to Adenauer could be particularly helpful in clarifying some of these matters.

The central theme of the conversation was the necessity that the United States, the leader of the Free World, have a faith and an ideal to guide other countries. Chancellor Adenauer felt that Russia's difficulties with China were just beginning, and that with the Common Market Europe was on the threshold of a new life. Therefore, there was tremendous potential on our side as long as it was harnessed and channeled in the right direction. He felt that the efforts that had been made to negotiate with the Russians, between Ambassador Thompson and Gromyko, were well worthwhile, although not immediately productive. He said it was important that the Russians realize that the United States, particularly, was willing to negotiate because the Russians, he said, had for many years genuinely believed that the United States was going to attack them. These conferences Adenauer felt would go a long way toward allaying those fears. France's refusal to participate in any of the negotiations and efforts obviously caused him anguish. It was the magnanimous gestures and efforts of De Gaulle himself that had permitted Germany to join the company of free nations, he said. It was De Gaulle who in 1958 offered the hand of friendship to him and it was this generous act that had culminated in the Common Market and the degree of unity that presently existed in Europe. "France's participation, yes, its leadership is absolutely essential," he said.

Chancellor Adenauer had a number of messages for the

President. He also did an extremely thoughtful thing for my mother, who, he learned, had attended a convent in Germany with her sister back in 1908-9. He sent a representative of his office to the school to search through all its old records, and then put together a scrapbook about the convent at that time. He presented it to me to give to my mother.

As we walked down to meet the other guests for lunch, we talked about the difference in our ages. He was fifty years old the year I was born. I asked him why he had stayed in government so long and why he was making the effort at his age. He said he had gone into politics and had remained in government because he wanted to keep Europe Christian and non-Communist. I asked him if he would like to change places with people of my age and whether he was optimistic about the future. He replied that he was optimistic but there were so many people being born in the world today he was just as happy that these immense problems were being faced by new generations.

At luncheon of trout and eggs we talked about the many political leaders with whom he had come in contact. He said of all the world leaders whom he had met during his career, the one whom he most admired was John Foster Dulles. In his judgment Dulles had the genuine faith in his convictions that was so necessary and so frequently lacking in the world today.

In my toast to Adenauer at luncheon I mentioned what an inspiration his career was to many young men throughout the world to serve their country and to perform that service with integrity and courage.

Adenauer is a politician in the best sense of the word. Although we did not speak the same language, I had the feeling I was talking to a real master in the field of political life. He made his points with a twinkle in his eye and it was obvious that this was an area of endeavor that he greatly enjoyed.

Interestingly, Chancellor Adenauer was not always held in such high regard by his friends and allies as he is today. While in Germany I learned of his responsibilities in the city of Cologne, which were terminated quite abruptly by the British in October, 1945. I obtained a copy of the letter that had been sent to Adenauer by the British General in charge of the area. I think the letter will give heart to all who at one time or another have not, in the eyes of their supervisor, been completely successful in the performance of their responsibilities—even if it is only clearing the streets.

HEADQUARTERS MILITARY GOVERNMENT
COLOGNE REGIERUNGSBEZIRK (808 DET.)

6 Oct. '45

Herr Oberburgermeister
Dr. h. c. K. Adenauer
Allianz Buildings
Cologne

1. I am not satisfied with the progress which has been made in Cologne in connection with the repair of buildings and the clearance of the streets and the general task of preparing for the coming winter.

2. About 2 months ago I personally warned you of your responsibilities in connection with this work. You have not fulfilled those responsibilities to my satisfaction. I am fully aware of the difficulties with which you have had to contend. I know that many of your colleagues have been removed for political reasons. I know the difficulties in connection with the labour situation in Cologne. I am fully alive to the position with regard to communication, shortage of coal, shortage of transport, etc. etc.

3. I am however convinced that with proper supervision and energy on your part, more could have been done to deal with these problems than has, in fact, been done.

4. In my opinion you have failed in your duty to the people of Cologne.

5. You are therefore dismissed today from your appointment as Oberburgermeister of Cologne.

6. You will leave Cologne as soon as possible, and in any case not later than 14th October.

7. You will immediately hand over the duties of Oberburgermeister of Cologne to the Burgermeister of Cologne Herr Suth.

8. Herr Suth will carry out the duties of Oberburgermeister of Cologne, as a temporary measure pending the appointment of an Oberburgermeister.

9. After you have handed over to Herr Suth you will take no further part in the administration or public life of Cologne or any other part of the North Rhine Province.

10. You will not indulge either directly or indirectly in any political activity whatever.

11. If you fail in any respect to observe the instructions contained in this letter, you will be brought to trial by the Military Court.

12. You will acknowledge receipt of this letter hereon.

Signed: BARRACLOUGH
Brigadier Comd. Military Government
North Rhine Province

Particularly notable, I think, is the fact that the British General, finding Adenauer not able to clear the streets properly, tells him, "You will not indulge either directly or indirectly in any political activity whatever."

The West German Society of Foreign Affairs is an organization very similar to the Foreign Policy Association of the United States. It is made up of leaders of the business and financial community, some of West Germany's most advanced thinkers in the fields of government and economics and others who are part of the West Germany power structure.

The most dynamic force operating in Asia today is the new nationalism of which I saw something in Indonesia. But in the Western world the most dynamic development of the postwar years is the Common Market.

The economic agreement among countries previously split by petty jealousies and historical boundaries promises to bring new wealth and economic stability to the participating nations and could indeed improve the condition of nations all around the world.

I felt, therefore, that this address offered a rare opportunity. For while the Common Market holds out great promise, it also imposes on those who take part tremendous responsibilities.

With this in mind I walked down the stairs into Beethoven Hall on the evening of February 24. My speech, in its entirety, follows:

"I come to Germany as a member of that national effort now under way in the United States which has become known as the New Frontier. Yet I do not feel, as I come among you, that I am passing from a new frontier to an old one; but rather that I am coming from one young and vital society to another of equal youth and vitality.

"For, if we in America are embarked—as I hope and believe we are—on a creative national effort, you are embarked on an undertaking even bolder in its departure from the precedents of the past. Your new frontier is nothing less than a new Europe, and I can assure you that all Americans salute the imagination and challenge involved in this immense project.

"This new Europe had its beginnings in the aftermath of the Second World War. Little has been more impressive in the years since 1945 than the recovery of Western Europe. Nations, ravaged and shattered by conflict, turned without discouragement or delay to the tasks of reconstruction.

"If the aid offered by the United States through the Marshall Plan made an indispensable contribution, that contribution could not have been effective without the hard work and intelligent planning of the European nations themselves.

"The result has been a veritable renaissance. By the early fifties, the rate of economic growth in Western Europe exceeded that of the United States as well as that of the Soviet Union. Economic recovery was matched by a revival of morale and creativity.

"Western Europe in the years after the war was not the predicted scene of exhaustion and defeatism. It was rather a scene of marked vitality, even exuberance—in science and technology and the arts even more than in politics.

"What was most impressive of all was the growing recognition that pride in nation was not incompatible with pride in Europe—that a person was no less a German or Frenchman or Italian or Scandinavian if at the same time he avowed his loyalty to the larger idea of Europe. Here the revival of Europe owes a particular debt to those statesmen who saw that Franco-German reconciliation lay at the heart of the European renaissance—and I have in mind especially, of course, General De Gaulle and your own great leader, Chancellor Adenauer.

"United Europe, first an idea, soon began to demand organizational expression. For a time this process was groping and fitful, at times even abortive. Often the failures seemed to have more impact than the successes. One recalls the regrets over the miscarriage of the European Defense Community.

"Yet, looking back from 1962, one sees a steady development and strengthening of European instrumentalities —from the OECD and the Coal and Steel Community to the rapid growth of plans and mechanisms in recent years. Today the European Common Market represents the culmination of the economic tendencies toward European union.

"I trust that you are in no doubt about the enthusiasm with which Americans have hailed the Common Market. We fondly regard it as an application to Europe of the principles which underlie so much of our own economic growth—the abolition of internal trade barriers, the enlargement of the internal market, and the consequent stimulus to production, innovation and efficiency.

"The announcement of Great Britain's intention to join only perfects the role of the Common Market as one of the vital centers around which the world economy will hereafter revolve.

"As yet, the new Europe has not found political institutions to match the Common Market. No one should be surprised at this. It is easier to reduce tariffs than to renounce sovereignty. Nor can an American be surprised that economic reciprocity precedes political federation.

"I recall that in our history it was the desire to remove obstacles to commerce between the thirteen newly independent American states which led to our Constitutional Convention in 1787, and not vice versa.

"One cannot foretell today the exact shape and structure of the political community of the new Europe. But no one can doubt that the will to a greater measure of political unity exists in Europe, and no one can doubt that in the end this will find its fulfillment in the creation of common political institutions.

"The potentiality of this new Europe is enormous. In population, in productive power, in the skills and talents of its people, in the wealth of its natural resources, in intellectual and cultural achievement and influence, the new Europe equals or surpasses even so great a power as the Soviet Union.

"The past contributions of Europe to the history of mankind are known to all; and there is no reason to suppose that these contributions will diminish in the future —so long as the new Europe can continually renew its intellectual and moral vitality.

"The new Europe exists. In this century it is a fact as massive and irrevocable as the awakening of the underdeveloped countries or the penetration of outer space.

"The concentration of population, skill, talent, wealth, knowledge and wisdom in this compact area is one of humanity's essential resources. No greater responsibility rests on the leaders of the New Europe than using this resource in ways which will renew the greatness of Europe, offering your traditions of leadership and creativity new fulfillment in a new age of history.

"You are the last people whom anyone need warn against the dangers of narrow nationalism. The record of European history is the world's strongest argument against a policy of isolation.

"Yet in troubled times there is always a temptation to grow one's own hedge and cultivate one's own garden. For either the United States or Europe to succumb to such a temptation would be unworthy of our past and unfaithful to our future.

"We cannot—you in Europe and we in the United States—become fortresses within ourselves, dealing with and helping only one another.

"If we do so, we will not be meeting our responsibilities to the rest of mankind, and very likely we will be spelling our own destruction.

"I come to Germany this time against the backdrop of many days' journey through Asia.

"I have seen men clambering out of stagnation and

squalor and demanding to be admitted to the twentieth
century.

"I have seen a new world beginning to emerge out of
centuries of oblivion.

"Half of the earth is marching out of the darkness into
the sunlight.

"It is a stirring experience to watch whole nations
struggling to achieve political independence and economic growth.

"It is stirring, and it is significant because the energies
released in this great historic movement—let us not mistake this—are going to reshape the world and determine
the future of man.

"In many aspects, of course, this world-in-the-making
represents a rejection of Europe and America. Yet nothing has impressed me more in recent weeks than the
extent to which this passion for independence and progress reflects Western values and Western purposes.

"If the new nations have repudiated European rule,
they have done so for European reasons. They are fighting for their new societies in terms of European ideals
of nationalism and democracy.

"It is their commitment to European doctrine which
has led them to reject European dominion. The ghosts
of Locke and Rousseau—and, if I may say so, Jefferson
and Lincoln—preside over the awakening of the East.

"The hope in these lands is to build modern societies,
blending their traditions and values with the achievements of Western science and technology—achievements
they are rapidly making their own.

"The end of colonialism does not signify the end of
a European role in these areas. The end of colonialism
opens rather a new era in the relationship between West
and East. It liberates Europe from old burdens and an-
tagonisms. It establishes the new nations on foundations
of self-respect and makes possible a new and constructive partnership in terms of common values and common hopes.

"The Western opportunity has never been greater. I
would add that this is not just a matter of opportunity;
it is a matter of necessity.

"It is in all our interests to narrow the frightening gap

144

between the rich nations and the poor, between people living in affluence and comfort and people scratching to survive on less than one hundred dollars a year.

"A high standard of living cannot remain the exclusive possession of the West, and the sooner we can help other peoples to develop their resources, raise their living standards and strengthen their national independence, the safer the world will be for us all.

"As President Kennedy said in his Inaugural Address a year ago: 'If a free society cannot help the many who are poor, it cannot save the few who are rich.'

"For thirteen years—ever since President Truman's prophetic Point Four speech in 1949—the United States has been devoting skills and resources to assist these new nations along the difficult road toward independence, self-respect and a decent level of life.

"We are proud of the contribution we have been able to make, but I would not be candid if I did not say that these contributions, when added to extraordinary expenditures required for the military defense of the Free World, have cost us heavily, particularly in our reserves of foreign exchange. This effort was a factor in the serious loss of gold which we experienced.

"Yet to default at this point would be to turn our back on the ideals which Europe and America hold in common, and it would be to deny the power realities of the world in which we live. Aid to the new nations of Asia and Africa and Latin America is an obligation for us all.

"Fifteen years ago, Europe could not hope to play its rightful role in the common undertaking. Today the new Europe, strong, vital and rich, must contribute both its wealth and its wisdom to this task. It must do so with generosity and with vigor.

"I am happy to note that Germany has recognized that its responsibilities increase as its capacity develops. The beginnings you have made on your foreign aid program are heartening.

"In 1961 I understand that you committed some $1.4 billion in economic aid to countries throughout the world. Other European nations have also increased their contributions. But we must continually ask ourselves whether this is enough, whether the terms of aid are sufficiently liberal and the magnitude sufficiently large to meet the needs of the developing nations.

"I would urge your thoughtful attention to this problem. We make the present uncertain and the future more difficult if we create the possibility of balance-of-payment problems for the new nations before they acquire the strength to surmount them.

"If we burden them with a heavy load of annual interest charges, we run the risk of stunting the very growth we are trying to promote. I am confident that you will agree that this vast problem can be met only with actions large in scale and generous in spirit.

"There is another area in which we must concert our efforts if the Atlantic partnership is to fulfill its purpose, and that is in the area of trade.

"Today we in America foresee a trading world radically altered in shape and size from any that we have known before. We observe the emergence of the new Common Market of America.

"Each of our Common Markets consists of a number of states surrounded by a common external tariff. There rests upon you and upon us the decision whether these revolutionary new arrangements will limit or expand trade for all the nations of the earth.

"President Kennedy recently asked Congress to grant him powers that would enable the United States, by agreement with the European Community, to bring about a substantial reduction in our common tariff and yours, for the benefit not only of the Atlantic partnership but of the whole Free World.

"We have taken this step in the confidence that we both can prosper by increasing the world commerce in goods and services. We believe that partnership, not protection, must be the watchword.

"The reduction of tariffs will, of course, involve readjustments for the United States in any such action; dislocations are inevitable, special interests will complain and painful accommodations must be made.

"This Administration recognizes these very real problems and is devising means of solving them. I anticipate a great national discussion of these matters this spring.

And I am convinced that, so far as my country is concerned, the leaders of business, labor and Congress will rise above particular interests and push forward in the interest of all.

"To America, the President's trade proposal is not merely a measure of commercial policy. It is a political act, designed to strengthen and consolidate the Atlantic partnership.

"If this new American policy is to be effective, the European Community must carry out the purposes it has set for itself. It must reject narrow nationalism and look outward to the world. It must aid and assist all less-developed nations, including former colonies and countries in Latin America and the British Commonwealth.

"It must be determined to bring about that expansion of commerce which can assure the most efficient use of our combined resources in a world where history has made efficiency an imperative.

"Just as the new Europe will fail if it turns into a white man's club, so it will fail if it turns into a high-tariff club. Our partnership can work and prosper only as it serves the larger interests of humanity; and as we serve humanity, we serve ourselves.

"We will not be diverted from our common undertaking by external pressures or external threats. Indeed, it is only as we fulfill our objectives of freedom and progress that we can defeat the Communist plan for mankind.

"The Communists know this perfectly well. That is why the effort to disrupt the new Europe has become a top priority of Communist policy. This effort springs from the ever more vivid contrast between Western Europe and Eastern Europe—between Democratic Europe and Communist Europe.

"The economies of Eastern Europe are starved and stunted; their societies pinched and unproductive; their cultures tense and bitter, looking constantly to the West for the replenishment of ideas and inspiration.

"Eastern Europe talks about internationalism and one economy; Western Europe accomplishes it.

"Eastern Europe talks about culture and art; Western Europe creates it.

"Eastern Europe talks about cooperation; Western Europe is beginning to practice it.

"It is against the backdrop of Communist Europe—drab, gray, monotonous, relentless—that the Communist assault on free Europe, and its variety and vitality and color, gains its particular bitterness.

"The attack on Berlin will be seen, in the long run, as the Communist response to the growing unity of Europe. Indeed, the essential contest between the Free World and the Communist world is which side can better manage its affairs, unite its purposes and concert its energies.

"There are indications today that, while the free states are working ever more closely together, the Communist system is beginning to exhibit signs of discord and fragmentation.

"Moscow says one thing, Peking another, and the still, small voice of Tirana compounds the clamor.

"This discord is the inevitable result of the attempt to impose a single policy on a world dominated by national traditions and national interests. It confirms our own view that the world is moving, not toward a single centralized order, but toward a unity in diversity, with many nations developing according to their own traditions and abilities. They remain bound by respect for the rights of others, loyalty to the world community and unshakable faith in the dignity and freedom of man.

"However, we must not rest on our oars. If the Communist system staggers, it is because of its own internal contradictions. We did not start this process, but we can accelerate it to some degree by steadily building our common strengths and remaining united in our common purpose of freedom.

"We can both look back with pride over the road we have traveled since 1946. But we must also look ahead, in the spirits of the new Europe and the New Frontier. For it is an unfinished society that we offer the world —a society that is forever committed to change, to improvement and to growth, that will never stagnate in the certitudes of ideology or the finalities of dogma.

"A hundred years from now there will be new ways

of making life better, of giving man fuller opportunity to fulfill his hopes.

"We have no infallible party, no iron creed, no all-purpose blueprint; we do not propose to chain mankind to a system of false logic. We have instead faith in human intelligence, human will and human decency; and we know that, in the long run, these are the forces which make history.

"Europe and America share great responsibilities to humanity. In meeting these responsibilities, we must both make a full commitment—not just to ourselves, but to the other members of the free community less fortunate than ourselves—not just of physical wealth, but, more importantly, of our minds and spirit.

"And with this commitment we may look forward in association with free men everywhere to the steady expansion of progress and liberty in the years to come."

A question period followed the address. One exchange may be of interest:

QUESTION: "Mr. Attorney General, you have pointed out the need for generous help to the underdeveloped areas and we certainly support it everywhere, but is there not this problem—that as we go along helping these areas we need strength and military strength as well for long periods, in order to be able to help them? Did you find during your journey that this interrelationship of the defense of Western Europe and the abilities of Western Europe to help the Asian nations was visible, was growing—or was it regarded as self-evident that we could help them generously all the time without getting any support in such fields as disarmament, as, for instance, the Belgrade Conference showed last August?"

MR. KENNEDY: "Yes, I would say that, first, among the leadership, in quiet conversation, there is complete realization of the necessity of a strong Europe and a strong deterrent force. I would say that in a number of these areas where this is never expressed publicly—and perhaps even to the contrary—it is expressed privately. A number of people, where there would be tremendous repercussions if it were known publicly, said to me for instance that if the Seventh

Fleet was ever moved they feel that it would spell disaster for them. And yet the public statements from that area of the world are continuously against the United States.

"I think that as they gain maturity and more confidence we can expect more from them. I don't think it's been very satisfactory. I would agree with you, and I think that all of us were disappointed with the Belgrade Conference. But I think that we can do better in the future. I think that there is a realization among the leadership of the importance of military strength, and I think that if we do the work among the young intellectuals that are coming along, and those who are being educated for the first time in their lives and who will be the future leaders of these countries—if we do the work and we sell our way of life—and, as I say, we have the truth on our side so it's a tremendous advantage—if we sell our way of life properly and if we work at it, we will prevail. I am far more optimistic after making this trip than I was before."

In Bonn, as elsewhere, we had an opportunity to meet and talk with a group of students. They expressed concern over what they feared was an anti-German sentiment in the world, growing out of World War II. They wanted to know about the strength of the U.S. commitment to West Germany and to Berlin. They asked plainly about disagreements between leaders of their own country and the U.S. Some of them had visited the United States. They said they found a lack of understanding on the part of our citizens about international affairs.

I was especially impressed with one young man who asked about our Peace Corps. This was not a new question, for there is considerable interest in this project. I explained something of its conception: how it had been an idea developed during the course of President Kennedy's campaign; how we had found many young people in the United States anxious and able to make a sacrifice for their country—but at a loss as to how they could be active; how the corps had developed after the election of President Kennedy. I discussed some of the good it is doing in many countries around the world.

But this young man was interested not only in what we in the United States were doing—he wanted to know if the young people of his generation in his country could possibly form a similar project. He said several organizations were considering such action and they needed stimulation. Several others in the crowd demonstrated interest. He promised to get in touch with the Peace Corps officials in the United States and I promised in return that we would provide the complete cooperation of our country's training methods and progress. This was just another example of the interest of youth universally to assume some of the responsibilities outside their own spheres, away from their own homes, beyond the frontiers of their own countries to help mankind.

They recognized a growing need for all of those who are fortunate enough to acquire an education to spread knowledge.

At the end of the meeting I told them I was encouraged by what they had asked and what they had said and what had been told to us by young people in other parts of the world. "For unless people such as you are willing to show an interest and make some sacrifices after you get out of college to help your government and to help other peoples in other areas less fortunate than your own, then you are going to have the young people on the other side, imbued with the philosophy of Communism, and willing to live and die for it, taking the lead."

From Bonn we flew to The Hague and then on to Paris, where I had a meeting with President De Gaulle. We talked about some of the same subjects I had discussed with Chancellor Adenauer. However, his position differed from Chancellor Adenauer's in that he was very concerned that the meetings in Moscow were even taking place. He believed nothing was going to come of them and that it was a mistake to meet with Communists when they were issuing threats. He said that his greatest concern was that the Germans would feel that their position was being undermined by these discussions.

I told him then that in conversation with me Chancellor Adenauer had said he was very pleased the Moscow meetings were in progress; that he felt they were worth the effort and that they had his full support. De Gaulle's reply was that meetings with the Russians should take place sometime, but only after the Soviet Union leadership had ceased their vituperation.

The conversation, although extremely friendly, was more

formal than the one I had with Chancellor Adenauer. De Gaulle's office was more austere, and whereas I had talked to Adenauer seated on a couch while he sat in a soft chair, my talk with President De Gaulle took place across his rather imposing-looking desk. However, I was impressed with De Gaulle's great vigor and determination. He made clear from the way he acted and the way he looked that he intends to be around for a long time to lead France to what he felt was her proper role in world affairs.

In conclusion, I told him how valuable the President felt it was to have a close working relationship with him and with France. I thanked him personally for the autographed picture that Jackie Kennedy had obtained for me from him after their meeting in Paris.

I thought, driving away from his office, what a tremendous contribution these two men, Adenauer and De Gaulle, had made to the cause of freedom. What figures in Eastern Europe are comparable to these two statesmen? It was another strong indication of the vitality and energy of the free way of life.

From Paris we flew back home. We had been gone just about four weeks. We were happy to be back.

CHAPTER 10

"... Let Facts Be Submitted to a Candid World ..."

—The Declaration of Independence

We arrived in Washington on the afternoon of February 28, 1962, from a trip which had taken us 30,000 miles to 14 countries in 28 days. We returned home with many thoughts and impressions, but one conviction stood out above all others: there is a tremendous reservoir of goodwill toward the United States which will disappear if the potential is not properly realized.

There is a deep undercurrent of affection and feeling toward the American people in the lands we visited. However, I strongly feel that what we do here in the United States—first, keeping ourselves prepared militarily, but also building our strength in the domestic areas, such as civil rights, economic productivity and Social Security—will have a major effect on our position in the world. The struggle we face cannot be won by waving a magic wand. It will take all our effort over the next two or three decades. It will exact a tremendous price. But it is a price we must pay, for if we do not succeed, we lose all.

Particularly in the field of civil rights, we must put our own house in order. In every country we visited, at every stop we made, in every community in which we met with students, labor leaders, or others, we were asked about civil rights in the United States. I told them of the gains that we made and the efforts of the Administration and the American people.

It is true that we have made progress, but there is so much progress to be made. It is true we are moving ahead, but we have yet so far to go.

One of the most elementary areas lies in the field of vot-

153

ing. When I came to the Department of Justice, in sixteen counties in the United States, Negroes outnumbered white people, and yet not one Negro was registered to vote. In dozens of counties in our Southern states less than 5 percent of the Negro population is registered. Major obstacles have been erected to prevent them from registering and participating in our elections.

Let me give just a few specific examples of unpleasant situations which create problems for this country—and also what we have been trying to do about them.

In 1960, a group of Negro citizens in Haywood and Fayette counties, Tennessee, where no Negroes were registered, formed an association for the purpose of encouraging their people to register and vote. Members of the white community retaliated by circulating lists of the Negroes who were attempting to vote, and urged their business associates to cut off their credit and fire them from their jobs. In spite of this, Negroes continued to try to register. White landowners then adopted a systematic scheme for the eviction of all their Negro tenants who were attempting to register to vote. By December of 1960 more than three hundred Negroes in just one of these counties had been ordered to move off their land by January 1, 1961.

The Department of Justice went to court to protect the right of these Negroes to exercise their franchise freely and without fear of retaliation. The court sustained our efforts and held that no one in the United States has a right to use his private property for the purpose of interfering with the right of a citizen to register to vote, or to penalize him for having registered.

Since then several thousand Negroes in Haywood and Fayette counties have registered. Biracial meetings are being held to discuss job opportunities for Negroes, and political candidates are actively soliciting support from the Negro community.

A similar sequence of events took place in the same year in a rural Louisiana parish. A Negro cotton farmer by the name of Francis Joseph Atlas, who had raised twelve children and given college educations to all but the youngest two (they were in high school), tried to register to vote. After several efforts he was told, when he took his cotton to be processed, that it would not gin. When he asked why, the ginner replied, "Civil rights." He then found that none of the other cotton ginners in the community would gin any more of Mr. Atlas' cotton.

Then the soybean processors refused to process his beans. Merchants from whom Atlas had purchased farm supplies refused to trade with him. The feed store manager told him he would no longer sell to him. They were literally trying to starve Atlas out of the community because he had the audacity to try to vote.

The Department of Justice also took this matter to court and asked for an order requiring cotton ginners and other merchants in Atlas' community to open the channels of trade to him on the same basis that they were available to other citizens. Under pressure from the court, Atlas gained the right to register, his cotton was ginned, and he is still farming in his community.

These are disagreeable events to discuss and record. Unfortunately, they are not isolated incidents. Threats, intimidation and legal manipulations are employed to keep the Negro from exercising his civil rights.

In one county Negroes whose exact ages appeared on their applications were denied registration because they inserted the phrase, "since birth," or "all my life," instead of the exact number of years, in the blank asking for the length of their residence in the county.

In another place Negro applicants who stated their names in four different places on one application form were rejected because they failed to insert it on the fifth blank.

Elsewhere, a Negro schoolteacher was rejected because in reading a long passage aloud perfectly, she pronounced "equity" as "eequity."

In another state applicants were required to fill in a blank labeled "color." Those who inserted "C" or "Negro" were rejected because only the word "brown" satisfied that registrar.

In one county in another state some Negro applicants were asked to explain "due process of law" to a registrar who had no legal training. None succeeded. None of the white people were asked a similar question.

In other counties we have found that Negro college graduates, university instructors, high school teachers and ministers were rejected by the registrar as being illiterate, while white people who had completed only the second or third grade were declared literate and allowed to register.

The Department of Justice is putting a major effort into eliminating such practices. They are the shame of this country.

As of January 20, 1961, at the time of President Kennedy's Inauguration, the Department of Justice was investigating or had brought court cases in connection with voting in only a few counties. By the first of May, 1962, action was taken in more than one hundred counties. However, the process is slow and cumbersome and the laws dealing with the problem are inadequate.

We have made a major effort to obtain legislation which would facilitate and expedite the handling of these cases; passage would have resulted in the enfranchisement of more than 500,000 Negroes. That effort was unsuccessful, but President Kennedy will make another attempt next year with similar essential legislation.

Throughout the government we are also exerting every effort to bring about economic as well as political equality of opportunity, and important work has been done by the President's Committee on Equal Employment Opportunity under the chairmanship of Vice-President Johnson.

This committee has been working for only a little more than a year. It has already signed agreements to insure non-discrimination with fifty-two leading employers covering some three million employees. These numbers should shortly reach almost ninety firms and five million workers. The results are apparent in many areas and this effort already affects large numbers of people.

Through this program Negroes have for the first time become production workers in a tobacco plant in North Carolina; they hold production jobs in an oil refinery in Illinois and a number of oil and chemical plants in Louisiana. Negro women have become seamstresses in a textile plant in South Carolina; Negro men hold metal-fabricating jobs in a Missouri plant, do production work in aircraft plants in Georgia and North Carolina, carpenter work in Florida, and now they are moving into electronic production jobs in Connecticut and Tennessee. These are just some examples.

So we are making progress in the areas of voting, transportation, federal employment, employment by government contractors, and also in other fields not directly related to civil rights which nonetheless have a major economic impact on Negroes, such as the minimum wage law, housing and the extention of Social Security.

But as long as inequities exist in the South, North, East and West, we have a task to perform. The Negro was called the White Man's Burden in the nineteenth century. Our treatment of the Negro is the White Man's Burden in this half of the twentieth century. We have to move ahead because our freedom, our strength, depend upon the maintenance of these ideals. We must advance if we want to fulfill our destiny and remain the leader of the Free World.

It may also appear incongruous to say that our foreign position will be determined by what we do to find employment for the miners of West Virginia, for the unemployed of the iron range of Minnesota, or for the 26 million young people who will join the labor market in the next ten years. But it is true. Furthermore, it is quite clear that our position throughout the world will be related to how we handle these problems, as well as the freedom riders or sit-ins or any others who are struggling for equality. If major progress is not made in these purely domestic areas now and over the next decade, our world position will be seriously shaken.

The leaders of the nations—of Asia, Africa, South America, the Middle East—during the sixties, the seventies and the eighties will be the intellectuals, the college students, the labor leaders of today. We cannot change their minds and interest them in democratic principles unless we are successfully practicing them at home.

When I visited Bonn, the first question asked by a group of German students was, "Why is the United States so unpopular with intellectuals and university groups, especially in Asia?"

This conclusion is widely accepted here in the United States as well as abroad. Certainly, it was my understanding before taking this trip. It is a verdict which I now believe to be completely unwarranted. However, unless we take major steps immediately, ten years from now it will be true. We must begin now to answer the cries that are raised against us.

An analysis of why there is a world-wide impression that our system is disliked can reveal to us the source of our difficulties, our problems and, also, some possible solutions. First, we must recognize that in each of these countries there is a strong and vocal Communist opposition to the United States and to our way of life. In all these countries this group is well organized. Highly disciplined cadres concentrate their activities in universities, student bodies, labor organizations and intellectual groups. Most frequently, their leaders are energetic, courageous and articulate. They have a party line they follow rigidly. They have fixed objectives, they know exactly what they think and exactly what they want. They know where they are going and they are willing to use any means to achieve their ends.

Within each of the countries, they exploit, frequently with devastating effect, the areas of differences between their country and the United States. In those countries which were formerly colonial possessions, the local inhabitants are apt to have an anti-European bias and the Communists are frequently successful in their efforts to associate us with that antagonism.

Beyond that, they take advantage of their nation's policy differences with the United States.

Communists vocally and actively back Indonesia on its position on West New Guinea. They claim that the United States' failure to support their position indicates the United States supports the Dutch and is, therefore, in favor of colonialism.

In Japan the Communists call for us to return Okinawa. Why, they contend, should we be occupying the Ryukyu Islands so long after the war? Again local sentiment is aroused against the United States.

Added to all this is the Communists' dedication. I think back to the young man who stood ten feet away from me at the University of Indonesia and hit me across the face with the piece of hard fruit. He was willing to risk prison to demonstrate his hatred for a representative of the United States.

Against this, as I saw repeatedly, there is no one to question their positions, their facts. There is no organization. There is no cadre. There is no disciplined and calculated effort to present another side.

And so it is that a small, able and well-trained unit can

take over a meeting or an organization, or even a government.

That was the important lesson of my experience at Waseda University. Approximately one hundred students, less than 2 percent of those present, were able to disrupt, disturb and almost cause chaos at this meeting. They did not want to hear a representative of the United States and they did all in their power to see that no one else did. They knew if they succeeded they would seize the newspaper headlines and the impression would be created once again that university students are antagonistic to the United States. The incident would be further evidence to the rest of the world that intellectuals in Asia are pro-Communist and opposed to America.

Of course, I do not claim that the rest of the students in the hall or outside in the courtyard supported the United States. Nor does the fact that there were no disturbances at Nihon University or Bandung or Jogjakarta indicate an acceptance by students at these universities of the American way of life.

But these students are not Communists, they don't accept Communism, and they have open minds. And this is what is important. They asked many questions about the policies and programs of the United States. Some of the points they raised implied fundamental criticisms of our role in foreign policy, of what we are doing in this country. By and large they were looking for facts—searching for information. They were hungry for knowledge, as were the vast majority of every student group to whom I spoke in other countries. The student bodies before whom I appeared were as friendly as any group I had ever addressed before, including any here in the United States. They are puzzled about many things in the United States and they want explanations. They hope the answers will give them the truth. But what they have been searching for has not been made available by us. True, we have given generously of economic aid, but the ideas and philosophies for which they hunger have not been forthcoming. They need—and want—more; it must be made available. A change in effort and direction is essential; we can no longer rely on purely material aid and expect that everything will somehow come out all right.

The amount of misinformation as well as the lack of information regarding the United States and our system of government in these countries is appalling. Many of the students and intellectuals think of the United States as it was fifty or even a hundred years ago. They know nothing of our social gains and little of the aims and aspirations of our people and our government. The Communist propaganda machine constantly spews out its facts and figures and its version of how to solve the problems of the world. It broadcasts the line that the Soviet Union and Communist China hold the correct philosophy and that the United States is always in error. The Communists in these foreign lands constantly build up the prestige of the Soviet Union. They talk about "the remarkable progress" Russia has made domestically. They boast about their achievements in space. The United States, on the other hand, to them is a system of "capitalistic imperialism," and everyone from Marx to Khrushchev knows just how cruel and aggressive that system is.

Colonialism is an evil, but as I learned from the student who introduced me at Bandung, colonialism and capitalism, and even imperialism, are interchangeable terms in the minds of many of these people. The United States is a capitalistic system and, therefore, the Communists can charge that the United States, given the opportunity, will seek to continue a system of exploitation. They, the Communists, are opposed to capitalism and, therefore, are automatically opposed to colonialism. These arguments obviously strike a responsive chord.

No one comes forward with an explanation of the modern-day United States; no one counters with the fact that modern-day colonialism is tied to Communism, not capitalism. No one is there to talk about Latvia, Lithuania, Hungary, Poland, Tibet or East Germany and East Berlin.

No one is prepared to counter the Communists' arguments with facts and figures. No one raises questions or stresses opposite opinions or positions. The Communists, for instance, have just boasted that Russia is going to provide its children with free schoolbooks. No one observes that the United States has been doing this for a hundred years. Or a representative of the United States arrives in a country to explain the American point of view. A small minority causes a riot, disturbs the performance or disrupts the speech. It makes the headlines across the world and creates exactly the impression the Communists wish to create—that students oppose Americans. On the other hand, a Communist comes to speak. Those who truly believe in the free system realize that opposition viewpoints should be aired. The Communist speaks, the audience listens, there is no display. Because of the contrast, the student body is thus pictured as disliking the United States and supporting Communism.

We are victims of a smart, articulate, well-organized minority which has kept us continuously on the defensive. We have permitted it to happen, we have allowed it to continue. If we do not meet the problem head on, if we are not ourselves imaginative, tough, dedicated, willing and self-sacrificing, the struggle with the enemy will not be won by them, but lost by us.

In Japan today there are more than 700,000 college students; in Indonesia there are approximately 75,000 where before the war there were only a few hundred; but the same situation is true in countries all over the world. In Honduras over 80 percent of the population is under the age of thirty-five. In Mexico and many of the other countries of South America, the figure is over 75 percent. These are the people who will be making the decisions in the next decade.

There is a great deal we can do to make available to them the facts about us and our way of life; to impress upon them that our system of government has made progress in the last fifty years; to let them know that our way of life is far different from what Marx described a hundred years ago; that this progress has been made under the banner of freedom. Fortunately, we still have time to take the necessary steps to win the fight for the minds of these young people.

In all these lands and with all these people, students, intellectuals and others, there is a profound unspoken admiration for America and American people. It was demonstrated over and over again—in kind words, the faces of children, the laughter of grownups. This reservoir is yet untapped; this is the tragedy of the past and the challenge of the future.

These are some of the basic things that we can do:

To all these nations, I would send groups of men and women to lecture, not just about the United States and our form of government, or about democracy generally, but also about history and philosophy and literature and even more practical matters.

JUST FRIENDS AND BRAVE ENEMIES

I would have people talk about some of the successes that we've had in the United States and the problems we have had to overcome. I would tell them more about what we have been able to accomplish. I would tell, for instance, about our farms and farm production. This area has largely been ignored. It is the backbone of any society. The failures of the Communist system are apparent while the successes that are being enjoyed in the United States and under the free system are extraordinary. In the free world we recognize the dignity and the worth of every individual and the aspirations he has to improve the living conditions of himself, his family, and his community. The individual is not just a cog in the state machine as he is when he lives under Communist control. History has recorded the deaths and the heartbreaks in the Soviet Union in the 1930's during the efforts to impose the Communist system. The newspapers have reported that hundreds of thousands of Chinese have been slowly starving under the collectivization program in the last years. Certainly comparisons can be made of the relative successes of the two systems. In the United States, for instance, a single farmer can cultivate more than three times as much acreage as a farmer on a collective or state farm in the Soviet Union. Furthermore, there is a tremendous contrast in the output per acre. The Soviet Union farm averages 21 bushels of corn per acre to our 55 bushels; 11 bushels of wheat per acre to our more than 26 bushels per acre. In the Soviet Union agricultural production has increased 30 percent from 1935 to 1939 while in the same period in the United States agricultural production has increased 70 percent. Most importantly, 48 percent of the labor force in the Soviet Union works on the farms and they are afflicted with many shortages. In the United States 8 percent of our labor force works on our farms and produces tremendous surpluses.

However, the story does not end just by contrasting the Communist system in the Soviet Union and the free way of life in the United States. Compare what has happened in Germany since she was partitioned—West Germany living in freedom and recognizing the individual, and East Germany existing under Communism with the individual reduced to a tool of the state. East German farms are now 20 percent below prewar production while West Germany is 41 percent

162

above. In virtually every commodity—wheat, rye, barley, oats, potatoes, to mention a few—West Germany outproduces East Germany in units per acre. These are only examples of what can be done and what has been done by men under a free system. We have not made sufficient effort to tell this story. And this is only part of it. *For the history of America—and, in fact, America today—is full of men and ideas that are far more exciting and revolutionary than the systematic, pushbutton answers of Communist doctrine. I would like to see more Americans making this point. By not doing so, we are leaving most of the world with the illusion that the only modern philosophy belongs to Marx. Mere anti-Communism is not a philosophy; it is no substitute for really knowing what this country is about. Its history, its philosophy, its political thought are all available. They just need to be used.*

Most importantly also, those we send abroad should go to learn, to listen and ultimately to report to the American people on the aims and problems of the people with whom they meet. They should make tours of as many universities as possible and should confer with labor leaders, farm and cooperative heads and government officials. Needless to say, the people sent should have a thorough knowledge of the history of the United States and the philosophy of our government and our people.

Many people more than qualify: Frank Church, Eugene McCarthy, Hubert Humphrey, Paul Douglas, John Sherman Cooper, in the Senate, to mention a few; Cabinet members such as Stewart Udall, Orville Freeman; and many members of the House of Representatives, and of our state governments, both Republican and Democrat.

Outside the auspices of the government, I would also like to see private citizens, such as some of our university professors, playwrights and poets, as well as articulate businessmen and labor leaders, travel under the same kind of program. I would like to see a man like Walter Lippmann or David Brinkley tour the Far East for a month, speaking on a number of subjects and answering the questions of students and intellectuals. They, like their government counterparts, in question periods and at appropriate times, should discuss the United States frankly, admitting our shortcomings, stating our efforts to overcome them, and pointing out this country's successes and accomplishments. We need people who have done their homework and who are not afraid to speak out.

I would have our government information agencies and services talk more about fundamentals in the United States. I would have them explain the social progress being made in this country, what people are doing for one another, what contributions altruistic organizations such as the United Givers' Funds, March of Dimes, and the Ford, Carnegie and Rockefeller foundations are making to the American way of life.

I would encourage other free countries of the world to set up their own "peace corps" with the understanding that our organization would cooperate closely with them. There is much, for instance, that young Japanese could do in Southeast Asia, and I am convinced that they would be willing to do it. Many of the young people in Germany, France and the Netherlands are as anxious as young Americans to help their fellow men in countries less economically fortunate. In all the students with whom I talked I found an idealism and a thirst to make the world a better place in which to live. This is a tremendous potential and it must be harnessed and utilized.

To make this kind of program effective or to give any of our efforts real meaning, I repeat that we must live up to our ideals within the United States. We will have a difficult time in selling students in Jogjakarta or Abidjan or Montevideo on our economic system if they read about coal miners in West Virginia being chronically unemployed. We will have difficulty in convincing intellectuals that our form of government is the most progressive if 6 percent of our working population cannot find jobs. It will be impossible to establish our way of life as the one being the most nearly perfect if the crime rate continues to rise four times as fast as our population rate.

And finally we must, despite the tragic disappointments of history and the agonizing betrayals of the past thirty years, constantly seek peace through controlled disarmament, while living with the bitter irony of the need for *present* military strength in order to maintain our freedom and that of other countries. This is a matter that is recognized by all. A high official of Indonesia, a country frequently critical of the